MORE THAN RUGBY

PENGUIN BOOKS

PIERRE SPIES

WITH MYAN SUBRAYAN

PENGUIN BOOKS

Published by the Penguin Group
Penguin Books (South Africa) (Pty) Ltd, 24 Sturdee Avenue, Rosebank, Johannesburg 2196, South Africa
Penguin Group (USA) Inc, 375 Hudson Street, New York, New York 10014, USA
Penguin Group (Canada), 90 Eglinton Avenue East, Suite 700, Toronto, Ontario, Canada M4P 2Y3 (a division of Pearson Penguin Canada Inc)
Penguin Books Ltd, 80 Strand, London WC2R 0RL, England
Penguin Ireland, 25 St Stephen's Green, Dublin 2, Ireland (a division of Penguin Books Ltd)
Penguin Group (Australia), 250 Camberwell Road, Camberwell, Victoria 3124, Australia (a division of Pearson Australia Group Pty Ltd)
Penguin Books India Pvt Ltd, 11 Community Centre, Panchsheel Park, New Delhi – 110 017, India
Penguin Group (NZ), 67 Apollo Drive, Rosedale, Auckland 0632, New Zealand (a division of Pearson New Zealand Ltd)

Penguin Books (South Africa) (Pty) Ltd, Registered Offices:
24 Sturdee Avenue, Rosebank, Johannesburg 2196, South Africa

www.penguinbooks.co.za

First published by Penguin Books (South Africa) (Pty) Ltd, 2011

ISBN 978-0-14-352816-6

Typeset by Nix Design in Adobe Garamond Pro
Cover by mrdesign
Cover photograph by Carla van Aswegen
Printed and bound by Ultra Litho, Johannesburg

CONTENTS

This book is dedicated to my parents: my mum, Deirdre, and my late dad, Pierre Spies Snr.

- Mum, you have been an inspiration to me and someone whom I respect tremendously. Thank you for making me see the importance of the basic things in life and for encouraging me to always remain true to myself.
- Dad, you have been the ultimate father and mentor. Thank you for raising us differently and instilling in us a sense of greatness. I'll always love you and keep you in my heart.

ACKNOWLEDGEMENTS

Rugby, Cricket and Soccer are team sports and so is writing a book. With a project of this nature, there are always people who play a role in making it all become a reality. I am deeply grateful to the following for their support and contribution.

First off, I want to thank my Lord and Saviour, Jesus Christ. He is 'The One' who changed it all, and made my life make sense, and who blessed me with all that I need and the hope to keep going.

My wife, Juanné. You are the most beautiful and unbelievable woman I know. Thank you for supporting me, picking me up when I'm down, and loving me and just making my life happy and fun. Thank you for always understanding and caring. I know that the best is yet to come: I can't wait for the rest of our lives together!

This was a huge family effort so, to my mom, Deirdre, and my sisters, Johanni and Steffani, who have been part of the making of this book since I was born. You are awesome women, and I honour, respect and love you very much. Thank you for being strong and courageous all through our lives together, and for being my sounding boards and anchors, keeping my feet on the ground. A special word of thanks to Johanni for all her hard work in getting this book right with our publishers, and helping to manage my personal and professional life at the same time. You were wonderful and I believe you'll achieve great things in life!

I want to thank my Uncle Dawie for his amazing contribution to this book and also to my life. Thank you for always encouraging me and praying for me. I believe you will go to great heights in life for the Lord.

My mentors, leaders and coaches, Pastor At Boshoff, Keegan Fredericks, Heyneke Meyer, Frans Ludeke, Johann van Graan and JJ Jackson. All of you have helped me so far and inspired me to keep going and to keep my eyes and arms towards the sky.

Victor Matfield, for writing the foreword. You are a true legend of the game and have been a massive help to my rugby and life. Thanks for being a great example. To Bryan Habana, Juan Smith and Morné Steyn, for also taking the time to contribute to this book. Without your words it would not be the same read.

My close friends, Ben Laubscher, Rudi Boonzaier, Didi von Staden, Walmar Slabbert, Deon Stegmann and Werner Kruger. Thanks for bringing normality and reality to my life. Joey Mongalo and Weber van Wyk, for their contributions to this book as well. Thanks, guys, for being there to offer me a shoulder to lean on and for just listening when I'm getting stuff off my chest or think I'm going crazy! I love you guys!

Myan Subrayan, my writer from Durban, now living in New Zealand. You have become a close friend in a short time. Thank you for encouraging me to put my story into a book and thank you for all the hard work you have had to put in on such a short time. You are an inspiration and motivation, and I know that God is planning huge things for you. I look forward to having that bunny chow with you. I know that you value your wife, just as I do mine, so to your wife Jolene, thanks for supporting Myan in all that he does.

Pastor Bert Pretorius and his church, 3C, for assisting Myan Subrayan during his time in Pretoria. I am truly grateful for the support you gave to make this all possible.

Geshana Nadesan and the rest of the team at Focus on the Family, South Africa. Keep up the great work you are doing to help grow and sustain healthy families.

I want to thank the whole team at Penguin SA for their professionalism in managing this whole book writing process, from inception to the finished product. Thanks also for your patience and great friendly service – its been so exciting to work with you guys!

Then YOU, the reader. Thank you for taking the time to read my story. May it offer a glimmer of hope in tough times, and may you also be inspired to write your own story. And may you keep on keeping on!

FIELD OF OPPORTUNITY

An open arena has always fascinated me. People with different backgrounds, beliefs and histories gather in a spirit of battle and competition. Different worlds come together at a stroke, when chance puts you in the seat next to your enemy, or else next to a motivated companion in battle, as if ready to be on the battlefield itself.

Battle commences and the war has begun. To and fro the battle goes, tipping the scales of fortune – either on the side of the better-prepared and physically more astute, or just favouring the lucky ones I guess … And still the spectators embrace the glamour and pain of what is happening in front of them.

The final blow is struck, the whistle has gone, and now it's no use trying or fighting, no use attacking the enemy with insults – victory belongs only to one: the one who kept going when time ran out, the one who endured the onslaughts and the damaging assaults of the enemy long enough, or the one who had a strategy that unfolded as if written in a book. Whatever the reason, whatever made the victor stand out, he's the champion: battle over.

Now the stadium is empty. In the arena of battle, the only sound is the stillness of nature. No warrior sneaking around for one last dash, no victory at stake – until the next time. The arena is at rest. Birds fly above, their calls echoing, and make their nests in dark, quiet corners. The debris of earlier excitement and indulgence is scattered across the arena, the mess of warriors and watchers waiting to be cleaned up.

The warrior is tired and bruised – but only until the next fight, where his fate will become a spectacle for the watching crowds, an entertainment to be remembered … or forgotten.

Luckily those days have changed, and we don't pay with our lives for losing a weekend game of rugby. But the spectators are still there, looking for excitement. People still place their hopes in their teams – they want to win! And who doesn't? The question, though, is, 'At what cost?' Victory isn't everything, that's for sure. And we can't get discouraged every time we lose. We prepare the best we can. On the day of battle, we make sure we're firing on all cylinders. We sleep enough and eat right – and when victory comes our way, we feel we've accomplished what we set out to do. But if we lose, we shouldn't lose heart or happiness.

Being in an empty stadium is really amazing. It is quiet; it's almost as if the stadium is making a sound of its own. It's a field of dreams, of champions, of stakeholders and shares – or a field of missed chances, injuries and bad decisions.

But most of all, it's a field of opportunity!

FOREWORD
BY VICTOR MATFIELD

I see Pierre Spies as a special person, on and off the rugby field. I really got to know him about five years ago, when he became a regular player for the Bulls during our 2006 season. Being one of the older players in the team, I thought that I was going to teach the younger players everything. My view changed instantly when I began hanging around Pierre. He is someone who came into the team as a youngster and has taught me and the team a lot, especially about life.

What I have learnt from Pierre has not necessarily come from his words, but more from his actions. One of the key qualities of Pierre that stands out for me is that he is someone who doesn't just 'talk the talk' but 'walks the walk' as well. For me that's very important, and as players we can vouch for the fact that he is consistent in his integrity, because we interact with him when the cameras are not rolling.

When we are on tour, Pierre is not someone who sits in his room the whole time. He is always interacting with the guys and being a positive influence. We all know that Pierre has a great love for God, and the other quality that stands out is that he never imposes his views on others. He doesn't shove his Bible down their throats, but instead he is an example by the way he lives his life, which the guys in the team see, and which draws them to him. This is what I believe makes a difference in peoples' lives: not just telling them how to live, but showing them how, by your own example. Pierre's actions speak louder than words.

A tremendous life lesson that immediately comes to mind is one he speaks about in this book: how he overcame the heartbreak of not being able to play for the Springboks in the 2007 Rugby World Cup, due to ill health. This experience would have been enough to devastate anyone, but not Pierre Spies. The way he maintained a positive attitude, despite seeing his dream to play in the World Cup fall apart in front of him, was simply inspiring to the rest of us in the team.

In the midst of this major setback, Pierre remained determinedly optimistic, which was hugely encouraging to those around him. I can remember my surprise and pleasure when he flew to Marseilles to hand out our match jerseys and speak to us before our quarter-final game against Fiji in that World Cup. Hearing him talk about the peace he had, despite the vast shadow of uncertainty hovering over his rugby career, was a great motivation for us. Through his example he taught us to be thankful for what we had, and to go out and give our best.

As you read this book you will share the same motivational and inspirational lessons that I and the rest of the team enjoyed from being around Pierre and observing him. It's great to have him in our team and he is genuinely an asset, on and off the field of rugby.

In my spiritual walk he is truly a figure I look up to. He is always the first guy to call us together on a Thursday or Friday to read the Bible, praise the Lord and just say thank you to God for everything He has given us.

I commend Pierre for so honestly sharing with us the many trials and challenges he has faced along his life's journey, and, more importantly, how he was able to overcome them. I was greatly encouraged, and I am sure that as you read this inspiring book, you will be too.

INTRODUCTION

By writing a book this early in my career, I may make people think that I'm boasting or being prideful. Let me say straight away that this is far from my intention. This book, as I have titled it, *Pierre Spies: More than Rugby*, is about my life journey up to now, and through it I want to provide hope and encouragement, and to show people that in life we all have to face our fair share of disappointments and setbacks. Life certainly doesn't have to end, our dreams abandoned, because of these problems: they are as much a part of life as anything else we have to undergo.

Right now you have the opportunity to use the talents you have been given, and a real opportunity to make a difference. Do you feel that you don't have any talents? Take it from me, we have all been given talents and gifts. These are things we are good at, which have been given to us for a reason, and that is to make a difference in the lives of others. Through this book I would like to inspire you to become all that you are capable of becoming, by using the talent that is within you. I will share some of my most personal successes and tragedies – and, more importantly, how they have shaped my life. I'm in no way a teacher or trying to show you how great I am. This is just my story so far. It's been quite a ride and I know that I'm a work in progress, like all of us. I also know that the best is yet to come – and isn't that exciting?

To the public eye my life might seem perfect, a bed of roses, and I don't deny that I'm living my dream: I've achieved my boyhood goals of playing for the Bulls and representing my country playing for the Springboks, and I've married the girl of my dreams, Juanné. As glamorous and attractive as all of this seems, the reality is that my life has been fraught with trials and tribulations. But in those moments when it seemed that life was treating me unfairly and not making sense, it is these words from my late father, Pierre Spies Snr, that motivated me and inspired me to endure and press on through whatever challenges I was facing at the time:

> The best is yet to come. That is what God wants for you – the BEST, to PROSPER.

These words are very special and mean a lot to me. My dad used to say them to me to instil the hope and courage that would enable me to face my tribulations. This is the essence of my book, to provide you with the same hope and encouragement I received. I certainly don't want to come across as an 'untouchable' or be seen as a religious fanatic. I just want to offer you whatever help I can by sharing my life experiences with you.

Yes, I admit this requires honesty and sincerity, and that's what you can count on with me: that's what you'll get. There are many personal accounts of difficulties that I have spoken about that we as a family have faced and overcome. By sharing these I accept that I could be exposing myself to criticism, and at the same time look as if I'm patting myself on the back. Is it worth it? I believe so, if it means helping someone. Constantly being in the public eye taught me very quickly that it's impossible to please everyone. So I have stopped trying to live up to people's expectations or seeking their approval. My life's foremost purpose is to please my Creator and to live according to His guidelines for me, as found in the Bible.

There is always a critic somewhere who will find fault with anything that you do. I was told that the only way to avoid criticism is to 'do nothing, say nothing and be nothing'. But that's certainly not the way I was raised, and it's not who I am.

Nor does the fact that I am 26 years old mean that I am too young to offer encouragement about life's challenges or to write a book about my life. The encouragement I offer is based purely on the challenges that I have personally faced. I am in no way claiming to be an expert or making myself out to be perfect, because I certainly am not. If I only shared with you the highlights of the success that God has allowed me to achieve, I would not be giving you the full, honest story of my life. I would be short-changing you, and I don't want to do that, because I promised you honesty. This will involve taking you behind the scenes, through my tough times as well as my good times, to understand the reality that in life we learn more from our losses than our victories.

That's right, what we think of as 'failure' is really life's lesson in how to succeed. As you read you will learn more of my 'life's lessons' and realise that as a sports star I am not excluded from hardships. The great thing is that I have learnt a whole lot from enduring and overcoming these hardships, and I am sure you will too. My mother taught me to never give up, to always be patient and persevere under hardship. It's advice that I think applies to everyone. Despite the challenges that life may throw at us, we have to choose to never stop believing in our dreams.

I am privileged and honoured to be able to journey with you through this book. Writing it has been a huge step of faith for me. I don't ever take my career for granted: I know it will eventually come to an end. In my line of work you are only as good as your last game, and your future extends as far as your next game. I am grateful for the privilege of being able to play rugby at the level that I do. Rugby is the platform that has enabled me to reach people with this message of hope.

Wherever you may be in your life journey, hold on to hope and believe that your best days are still ahead of you – that's what I do!

CHAPTER 1

Where it all began

There is no doubt that it is around the family and the home that all the greatest virtues, the most dominating virtues of human society, are created, strengthened and maintained.

Winston Churchill

In all that I have learnt thus far, one thing that has always stood out for me and that I value a lot is the importance of family. This truth was imparted to me as I grew up and is something that I cherish and hold dear to this day. It is a very well-known fact that you can choose your friends, but you cannot choose your family.

Based on my passion for family and all the good that it stands for and promotes, I wanted to start my book by highlighting the importance of family and the role that a healthy family plays. Please don't think that I'm gloating or boasting about how great my family was (or is), because I'm not. As you read, I will share with you the major setbacks and challenges that we had to endure together as a family. Through all of these impediments that we faced along the way in the Spies family, I can confidently say that we have remained a close-knit family. We have not allowed life's difficulties to break us up or cause us to drift apart, but rather have let them bring us together.

It's my firm belief that no matter what, a family must stick together.

I cannot imagine what my life would have been like without the loving support of my parents and my sisters. For most of my childhood, I was truly blessed to grow up in a loving home. I stress 'most' because, as you will soon find out, our loving home was to be split apart. And you will also learn of the devastating impact this had on me and the rest of my family.

Part of my reason for writing this book is to clear up any misapprehension that, because I might be seen as a professional sportsman, everything was handed to me on a plate, or that my life has been pretty easy. I can assure you that as I was growing up, my life was nothing like a fairy tale with a guarantee that I would live 'happily ever after'. Even though both my parents committed their lives to a full-time Christian ministry of serving God and His people, as a family we had our fair share of adversity. Because family is a subject that is so close to my heart, please indulge me as I set out my interpretation of 'family'.

I believe that the family is the basic building block for all society. When we consider the make-up of society in general, it is not hard to see that the family is undoubtedly the foundational component upon which any society rests. It is my firm belief that it is the lifelong commitment of a man and a woman that allows families to be created and held together.

'Family' defined

In coming together through marriage, a husband and wife choose to cooperate to raise and nurture the children born to them. Strong families are the building blocks vital to the development of any community, and there are many benefits derived from the values and nurturing of strong families. Among the pivotal advantages are the strong social structures that arise from the family unit.

A very wise South African, Archbishop Desmond Tutu, said:

> You don't choose your family. They are God's gift to you, as you are to them.

I strongly agree. I believe that this is how we need to view our family, irrespective of their faults and shortcomings.

With all of this said, let me go on and share with you what it was like to grow up in the Spies family. My elder sister Johanni, younger sister Steffani and I were instructed in the ways of God by our parents and learnt to always place Him first. In those early days we truly basked in the love of the Lord and I felt blessed. Through our close-knit family and the love we shared for each other, I started to comprehend, from that young age, the loving kindness of a caring Father in heaven. My dad was a blessed individual whose every action expressed his gift of encouragement and motivation. He brought us all up to believe that we were special and different. He and Mum taught us to believe, from birth, that God had created us with a plan and that Jesus was the way, truth and life.

A great sense of excellence and greatness was instilled in us from a very early age. Words like 'unbelievable', 'amazing' and 'extraordinary' were part of our family's everyday vocabulary. These are words that don't get used often in every household, but we grew up believing that we could be or become the best at whatever we set our hearts on. My dad certainly did raise us to be different, and a large part of our upbringing was based on the strong foundation of the Bible. It was my dad's motivation, his source for the way he brought us up.

Our parents raised us to remember Scripture passages, and in my solitary moments I would scan the Bible for short verses to memorise. I would commit them to memory, building up my strong Scriptural foundation. Dad was always big on hugging, kissing and expressing his love and encouraging us.

My dad had already established himself in the Northern Transvaal 'Blue Bulls' rugby first team, playing in the number 14 jersey as an outstanding right-winger. He was also a South African athletics champion in the 110 metres hurdles. Such was his tremendous talent that in 1975 he broke the African record for this race when he was clocked at 13.5 seconds. My dad, in the words of many people who knew him, was a 'legend'.

Dad was strict but always positive. He instilled in me the fact that I was the best, and motivated me regularly by telling me that hard work would take me to the top. Mum provided a good balance and taught us that relationships with people were what would take us through life: we had to be disciplined and walk in truth with ourselves and people. The two of them gave us a great combination of lessons for life. My dad was an amazing person whom people loved being around. At family gatherings he always took centre stage as people gravitated to his charisma and character. I was different: I was quiet and reserved, while he did all the talking.

I remember that he always bragged about us. Even in his role as a motivational speaker he would tell people about his kids. He said he did that to show other people that they also needed to be proud of their children and speak well of them.

There is so much more I could say about him, but I will keep that for a later chapter. I wouldn't be doing his legacy justice if I left it at this.

My beautiful sisters

Let me start with Steffani. She was an amazing athlete at school and had my dad's hurdling style. Her personality is very different from mine and Johanni's, and she is the harmoniser in our family. Always trying to make sure everyone is having a good time and that everyone is OK – she's also very funny! She is married to a farmer, PD, who's currently playing rugby in France. (They got married two weeks after me and Juanne!) My other sister, Johanni, is the strong one and a typical eldest child, being really responsible and disciplined. She did ballet and plays the piano really well. She didn't have the same athletic abilities (she was more cultural if you know what I mean) as me and Steffani, but she always worked just as hard at whatever she did. She is a great motivator and also works for me in managing my deals and endorsements, together with my agent.

My parents met in 1975 just after my dad became a Christian and gave his heart to Jesus. Mum was only 15 at the time, and he was 24. They met in church and were drawn to each other by their common desire to serve God, and the fact that my dad couldn't keep his eyes off my mum! In 1977 my dad was able to merge his two great loves at the time, sport and God, when he formed Sportsmen for Christ. He and his fellow members travelled the length and breadth of South Africa, giving their testimonies and sharing how God had made a difference in their lives. He also worked as a marketing rep for a sports goods company. In 1978, after four years of courtship, Pierre Snr and Deirdre were married. My dad shared these words, which had motivated him to ask for her hand in marriage:

> May the Lord make your love grow and overflow for each other and everyone around you.[1]

By today's standards there was quite a big age difference between them, but according to Mum, Dad was her hero, and she felt the same way he did. 'He was the man I wanted to grow old with, and I knew that it was from God and not a hoax.' Their first child, my eldest sister, Johanni, was born in 1979, followed by my other sister, Steffani, in 1982, and by me, Pierre Johan Spies, the third child and only son, on 8 June 1985. My mum told me that there was always a very special bond between a mother and her first-born son, and that's exactly how it was with us. She said that when I was born, when she first held me, she knew that I had a special blessing over my life: 'This child was given to me to raise him up in God's ways, but he would not belong to me as he was born for a greater task.'

Mum told me that on the day I was born, she got this special promise about me:

> My child, never forget the things I have taught you.
> Store my commands in your heart.
> If you do this, you will live many years, and your life will be satisfying.
> Never let loyalty and kindness leave you!
> Tie them around your neck as a reminder.
> Write them deep within your heart.
> Then you will find favour with both God and people,
> and you will earn a good reputation.
>
> Trust in the LORD with all your heart;
> do not depend on your own understanding.
> Seek his will in all you do,
> and he will show you which path to take.
>
> Don't be impressed with your own wisdom.
> Instead, fear the LORD and turn away from evil.
> Then you will have healing for your body

and strength for your bones.
Honour the LORD with your wealth
and with the best part of everything you produce.
Then he will fill your barns with grain,
and your vats will overflow with good wine.[2]

My mother taught us the art of survival, which is to live with endurance and perseverance. She taught us diligence and nurtured a fighter's spirit within each one of us: never give up in challenging times, and have patience and perseverance. According to Mum, she and Dad became so involved in full-time ministry that they never had much time for things that were outside the church. The ministry they worked in was an international, interdenominational one called Campus Crusade for Christ. This happened after my dad had visited the United States of America in 1981, where he met with the crusade's leaders.

On his return from the USA, he started the South African branch of a Christian sportspersons' organisation called Athletes in Action. It was a part of Campus Crusade for Christ and focused on using the life stories of well-known sportspeople to encourage people to live godly lives. My parents served in this ministry for nine years and then started another called Word in Action, also interdenominational, which focused more on families.

Dad also ran a ministry called Camps for Men in the Mabula Game Reserve, where we had a family holiday home. He held these camps, which used to attract up to 250 men at a time, from 1989 to 1997. Later in this book I share an account from one of these particular camp meetings where Dad used me to highlight an important truth to those men about being a father.

Dad was a teacher of biblical truth, and didn't see himself as a priest or pastor, as that calling didn't attract him. He felt that being ordained would hinder the freedom he had to travel and minister to people around the country. I have been told by many ministers that my dad was a pioneer of these Christian camps for men in South Africa, and it is great to see that the spirit of these camps is still alive and well in the country and that more men realised their dependence on God through Angus Buchan's Mighty Men's Conferences over the past few years.

Being in full-time ministry, my parents had to rely on donations and sponsorships to meet their living expenses, so generally they lived by faith. They had no regrets about this, as they said it taught them to trust in God for everything.

Having been exposed to Christian ministry for the greater part of our lives, my sisters and I were well versed in the Bible and in God's ways, and we learnt to always place God first. As I've already mentioned, my parents encouraged us to memorise Scripture, and we were taught to trust in the Word of God from an early age, learning it verse by verse and reciting it to guests visiting our home – Dad would call us and we would have to stop what we were doing and tell the people our verses – always doing it gladly.

My recital Scripture, which I remember rehearsing over and over again, was Psalm 1:[3]

Blessed is the man
Who walks not in the counsel of the ungodly,
Nor stands in the path of sinners,
Nor sits in the seat of the scornful;
But his delight is in the law of the LORD,
And in His law he meditates day and night.
He shall be like a tree
Planted by the rivers of water,
That brings forth its fruit in its season,
Whose leaf also shall not wither;
And whatever he does shall prosper.
The ungodly are not so,
But are like the chaff which the wind drives away
Therefore the ungodly shall not stand in the judgment
Nor sinners in the congregation of the righteous
For the LORD knows the way of the righteous,
But the way of the ungodly shall perish.

I was a happy child and was experiencing God's true blessings in my life. My parents loved each other and protected and challenged us at every level – always offering their support and motivation. From a young age I learnt to comprehend the Father's heart for His children here on earth. My dad played a huge role in this, and I am truly grateful to him for also instilling in us a strong champion spirit, teaching us to believe that we are winners.

CHAPTER 2

Going back to grassroots

We shall not cease from exploration
And the end of all our exploring
Will be to arrive where we started
And know the place for the first time.

T S Eliot

I can remember that I didn't take too kindly to losing in my early pre-teen years. In fact, I was a very bad loser, and I'm not exaggerating at all! Whatever game I was playing, if I lost, I would stop and begin to cry. Now you tell me: how bad was that?

I always thought I was the best and didn't want to lose. It may have been thanks to all my dad's encouragement to me to excel and win that I assumed I had to win at everything. I expected it so much that I wouldn't accept losing. Or more probably I just had no idea how to accept defeat gracefully. I thank God that I matured and learnt that life is not always about winning. Sooner or later we have to face the fact that we might lose at something.

I recall an incident when I was ten years old that reflected this poor attitude of mine. My dad and I had been playing golf against my cousin Stephan and his father, my dad's brother, and I had lost to my cousin. Because I was so upset at losing, I refused to finish playing the last hole. I charged straight to the car to sulk and cry like I've just lost the US Masters. My dad came over and told me to get my act together and 'get over it',

as I was making a fool of myself. He then made me come back to the
clubhouse for a drink with them. I was glad that my cousin, who was a
year older than me, acted more maturely than I did and didn't rub in the
fact that he had beaten me. Today we still play golf together – but not as
competitive as back then!

My dad's advice helped me accept losing and become a good, gracious
loser. I remember recently hearing a saying that goes something like this:

> You show some of your character when you win, but all of
> it when you lose!

It's a great feeling to win, but the reality is that you're not going to be on
the winning team all the time. Being a slow starter, I didn't excel at sports
in my primary school days, except towards the end. It was really at high
school that my potential began to show. This was largely due to the effort I
put into training hard and working at my training programme.

Before I donned a Bulls or Springbok jersey, I played for my school.
I may not have been as talented then as I am today, but it was a start to
getting me where I am now. To get to the heart of my rugby journey, we
need to take a trip down my grassroots rugby lane. As I begin thinking
back on my schooldays, I'm grateful to all the passionate teachers and
coaches who invest their time and energy in sports. It is their efforts that
give young players a chance to compete in sports of all kinds.

A valuable quality that school rugby teaches you early on is discipline
– though I know of one school, at least, that took it a bit far, although they
enjoyed the rewards for sure. Paarl Gimnasium, where one of my teammates, Springbok centre Jean de Villiers, was in the Under-15A side, insisted
upon the reinstatement of the cane to enhance their performances. They
even gave it a name, Daisy. For two years, Daisy saw to it that concentration
levels were at an all-time peak, and that no rugby ball was ever dropped.
Not surprisingly, the team went unbeaten for those two years.[4]

I'm sure the schoolkids reading this are saying an emphatic no to such a
method of instilling discipline, while the dads are probably remembering
when it was all part of the school 'learning experience', and saying, 'Bring
back Daisy!' Well, kids, aren't you glad that times have changed and you

don't have to contend with canes?

More than discipline, it was also at school that I developed lasting friendships that I still enjoy today. In my early schooldays I also learnt the value of the team, and of the game itself, and how it needs to be played together, with forwards and backs working towards a common goal.

Jake White, the former Springbok coach, still has an affinity for school rugby and gives this grassroots level of the game high praise:

> Rugby is a game where the players are tested – intellectually, physically and emotionally. At the great schools scattered around our country this game is learnt and played in a context of an educational package. It is part of what will mould the young men involved into mature young adults … I can confidently boast that South Africa has the healthiest reserves of young, raw talent anywhere in the world. The success of the Springboks is directly related to this.[5]

Primary school

In primary school I excelled as both scholar and sportsman. After Grade 1 at Laerskool Pretoria-Oos (Pretoria East Primary School), I moved to Skuilkrans Primary School in Murrayfield, where I finished my primary schooling, except for my Grade 5 year, which I spent at Nylstroom Primary School. At Skuilkrans I became head boy and received the dux award for versatility.

I went to Nylstroom because it was near to the Mabula Game Reserve, where my parents ran the camps I mentioned earlier. Because we spent so much time there, my parents thought it might be a good idea for us to live near the game farm. I stayed at the high school hostel although I was only 11 years of age, so I learnt the facts of life much earlier than I should have, and from the older high-school boys. I remember coming home and telling my mum the dirty jokes I had heard in the hostel, and seeing her jaw drop. Innocent and immature as I was, I thought they were really funny – but apparently they weren't.

Living in the hostel wasn't all that bad, as my cousin was there too, and we shared a room. My sisters were at the high school, which saved me from being bullied. No, they didn't beat up any of the bullies, but their good looks came to my rescue. The older boys knew that if they wanted to go out with either of my sisters, they had to be nice to her little brother – me!

When I was in Grade 7, aged 13, I went to the provincial athletics trials and came last in hurdles, shot put and javelin. That's right, this is not a misprint – I came last! Nothing like the results I would achieve in my last year of high school. Despite my poor performance I clung to my dad's advice and was sure that the best was yet to come. I was definitely what you would call a 'late starter'. Physically and biologically I was a bit behind: I noticed that all the other boys my age had hair under their arms and were bigger than me.

I recollect that I started rugby when I was around eight years old. I played wing, centre and then eighth man, as that's where I wanted to play. My primary-school hero was the juggernaut All Black left-winger, Jonah Lomu, whom I thoroughly enjoyed watching break tackles and score magnificent tries. I was glad, though, that the Springboks were able to contain him and win the 1995 World Cup. But, boy, did I enjoy seeing him play against England in that World Cup! I was such a big Jonah Lomu fan that on my mum's birthday I made her a birthday card full of pictures of him running with the ball.

My idols during high school were the England ace kicker Jonny Wilkinson and our very own Bob Skinstad. Thinking about it now, I realise that by the time I got to high school, I was more a fan of playing rugby than of watching it on TV.

I went on to captain our primary school's first rugby team when I was in Grade 7. For one game, we were so psyched up that I recall most of us being in tears as we ran onto the field. This was certainly not the norm for primary-school rugby back in those days. But the pre-match mental preparation paid off: I recall scoring a try in that game, and we went on to win. The after-match get-together for all the kids and their parents was at a local restaurant, and one of my mate's dads kindly picked up the tab for us all. I recall my dad urging me to go up to him, thank him for paying the bill and give him a hug, which I did in appreciation.

Another thing I remember about that victorious game was how proud my dad was of me. For the whole game he stood cheering from the sidelines, supporting and encouraging us. He would also do the customary 'chirping' at the referee to make sure he was doing a good job. It was nothing malicious or nasty, just something like, 'Ref, where's your guide dog today?' As I look back, I realise how much it meant to have my dad supporting me from the sidelines. Knowing he was there watching made me put in that extra bit of effort. Dads and mums reading this, please take note of what an impact it has when you are there to support your kids on their game days. Take it from me, it means a lot! You don't have to do anything special: your mere presence means a lot and gives your children so much encouragement.

That's one of the many things I appreciate about my dad. He always made the time to attend my games, no matter how busy he was. I am also grateful to him for teaching me to obey and respect my parents. I just knew that this was right, from the way I would observe him respecting his parents. It is common knowledge that children follow the examples of their parents, and not just their advice. I believe it is imperative for parents to live their lives as an example for their children to follow. Also, it is crucial for parents to respect themselves first, in order to succeed as an example for their children. I like this:

Children shut their ears to advice and open their eyes to example.

Even though my parents were starting to go through tough times in their marriage I chose to respect and honour them, which I believe is the right thing. I may not have agreed with what they were doing, but I chose to obey the Bible and respect them.

High school

After primary school my dad enrolled me at the Afrikaanse Hoër Seunskool (Afrikaans Boys' High School), in Pretoria, better known as 'Affies'. At first I didn't want to go there, because all my friends were going to Hoërskool Die Wilgers. But Dad knew what was best for my future in rugby, and

Affies has a great rugby tradition, so I'm glad he insisted that I go there.

Making the transition from primary to high school is always tough in the beginning. I was overwhelmed by the size of the high school and the vast numbers (to my eyes) of students. For the first two weeks we had to endure the traditional initiation process, which included 'holding the wall',[6] and having to wear our primary-school uniforms. When you could at last put on your Affies uniform, you were really proud. All in the name of tradition. In the beginning I didn't like being at Affies as there were lots of cliques and I was in the minority. Two of my primary-school friends who were there too left and went to Die Wilgers. The jump to Affies was a bit too much for them to handle.

In this time, things started to change for me. I was going through the typical changes a teenage boy experiences – like wanting to impress the girls but feeling insecure. Physically I looked terribly out of proportion, with extra-large ears and feet. Classic teenage skin problems didn't help my confidence levels one bit. I didn't play for the A team, and wasn't popular. The good thing was that my attitude was right, and I always participated in as many events as I could, knowing through what my dad had taught me that hard work and a good attitude are what pull you through.

My dad always emphasised this:

> It is not how you start, but how you finish. Life is all about finishing strong!

Here is a table that plots my rugby progress during my high-school years:

AGE	TEAM LEVEL	POSITION	COMMENTS
Under-14	B team	Eighth man	I was captain. Tough season and didn't enjoy my rugby as wanted to play A team.
Under-15	Started off in B team and then moved to A team	Wing and lock	Started playing really well, resulting in me moving up.
Under-16	A team	Lock	Did well and went on to Bulls Under-16, playing with hooker 'Chiliboy' Ralepelle.

My dad used to tell me during the games I had to try to get myself into good positions, as my strength was having the ball in hand. Even when I played lock and was the tallest in my team, I still had these playing skills. I was a very good lock and played like an extra loose forward when I was under 16.

I can remember one specific run that resulted in me being selected for the Under-16 Blue Bulls team. It was during the school trials, and it was from a 22-metre kick-off on us. I went back, something that locks didn't normally do. The opposition, seeing this, kicked on me. I caught it and just 'flooded' it, and made some really good yards, which impressed the selectors. I most certainly believe it was that run that got me selected into the Blue Bulls Under-16 team.

During my high-school years I befriended a great guy, Weber van Wyk. He and I are really good friends to this day. Because it's hard for me to remember everything about my schooldays, I called him up and asked him for a contribution to this book. Here it is.

Weber van Wyk
Friend

'No one would think that a lock could catch a wing, but that was Pierre for you: an all-round brilliant player.'

The first time I really got to meet Pierre was when we were together in high school at Affies. Pierre and I competed for the same position at under-14 level. My first impression was that he was too thin to keep me out of the team, which everyone can clearly see has changed over the years. Both of us were keen competitors on the sportsfield from a young age, but that didn't stop us from getting on well from the day we met.

Pierre came from a family of brilliant sports figures, which probably put pressure on him to succeed, although his family never put pressure on him to do well. His own determination and will came through early, in the way he approached everything he did, from being number one in the country at throwing the discus to being one of the best schoolboy rugby players. He always went the extra mile when it came to training, and I think that still separates him from the rest. I have no doubt that Pierre is a hard worker and earns everything he achieves.

Everyone is probably familiar with the many great games Pierre has played for the Bulls and the Springboks, but let me mention one or two that I will always remember from our schooldays. One was the Under-16 *Beeld* Trophy final against Zwartkop High School. Pierre was playing lock for our side, and it was a very intense game, with neither team able to get over the try line. Zwartkop had a wing, Marius Delport, who currently plays Super 15 rugby for the Lions. Marius got the ball and was well on his way to scoring a try in the corner. Pierre, who was a lock forward then, chased him all the way from the line-out and caught him in the corner, before he could score the try. No one would think that a lock could catch a wing, but that was Pierre for you: an all-round brilliant player.

Then there was the game against Bishops in our final year. We were behind, just before the final whistle, when Pierre intercepted the ball on our 22-metre line and sprinted all the way through to score the winning try. There was no doubt in my mind, even in those early days, that Pierre was destined for greatness.

As an old school friend, I know that the serious Pierre Spies we are so used to does have a lighter side too. We had a couple of funny experiences together at school, and I only need to mention one of them to prove that Pierre is a fun guy.

When we were both 17, we toured the Eastern Cape with the school's first rugby team. One night, after a braai – it was around one o'clock in the morning – Pierre and I decided to visit a couple of girls we had met earlier. But the place where they were staying was not within walking distance, so we had to make a plan. We knew the coaches had a rented car, and we had to get a hold of the keys. We were so determined that we climbed over two walls to reach the coaches' apartment.

The assistant coach was Johan van Graan (today the Bulls forwards coach). We peeked through the window and saw him fast asleep, the keys next to his bed. Silently we opened the sliding door and took them – but then he woke up. We froze. When he asked us what we were up to, we told him we just wanted to see if he was awake to join us for the braai (which had actually finished more than two hours earlier). Luckily he chose to go back to sleep and we were out of there – with the car keys! Pierre was the better driver, or at least he was confident about it, so he took the wheel. We visited the girls as planned, came back at three o'clock, safely returned the keys and went to bed.

The next morning, as we were all standing outside, Johan got into the car and immediately realised someone had pushed the driver's seat back as far as it would go. It took him a while, but eventually he put two and two together: he remembered that we had been in his room and that Pierre had the longest legs in the touring party. He just looked at both of us and smiled – and we knew we'd been caught out.

A lot of people don't know it, but Pierre has a great sense of humour and is always keen to tell jokes. Yet he can also be a very serious guy, and will do anything for his family and friends.

Someone I met for the first time the other day told me that Pierre's DVD had made him look at life in a completely different way. To have a friend like Pierre, with such a passion to make a difference in people's lives, is a great privilege. I admire the way he keeps his humility while doing this great work. Pierre might not be aware of it , but there are many, many people who see the wonderful things he does, and the passion he has for God, and admire him for that.

Thanks, Weber, for sharing this. I just hope we don't get into trouble now for taking Johan's car that night! You've got to understand that Johan, as Weber mentioned, is my current forwards coach at the Bulls, so I hope that he doesn't still hold it against me and put me on the bench for the next game.

In 2002, at 17, I was selected to play at the Craven Week provincial schools tournament. It was here that I met Joey Mongalo, and we became good friends. He was at Pretoria Boys' High School and played scrum half. We shared a hostel for that week, and would stay awake at night, talking about girls, life and all the usual things teenage boys speak about. We even spoke about our faith, though we weren't committed about it. At that tournament we were all given a book called *Prayer of Jabez*, by Dr Bruce Wilkinson (Multnomah, 2000).[7] It said that God would enlarge our 'tents and territories'. Little did I know how prophetic the message of that book was going to be in my life. Our chaperone did Bible study with us, and I recall Joey and me asking a lot of questions, as we were young and had enquiring minds. But I'll give Joey a chance to speak for himself in the next chapter.

The great thing about the Word of God is that it accomplishes what it is purposed to do and doesn't return void.

For as the rain comes down, and the snow from heaven,
And do not return there,

But water the earth, And make it bring forth and bud,
That it may give seed to the sower, And bread to the eater,
So shall My word be that goes forth from My mouth;
It shall not return to Me void,
But it shall accomplish what I please,
And it shall prosper in the thing for which I sent it. [8]

I didn't feel that I had a good Craven Week in 2002, as I was in bad shape. I was unfit and weak, and I was partying a lot, which certainly didn't help with my fitness. It was after that 2002 Craven Week that I started training very hard. And that was also about the time that my sister Johanni fell pregnant, which I will speak more about later.

In the 2002 national athletics championships I threw the 1.5 kilogram discus 61.18 metres, which was the fourth-furthest distance ever thrown by an under-17 athlete at the time. This resulted in me qualifying for the World Junior Championships, but I didn't go as they were held at the beginning of the year, when we played rugby. My rugby was more important to me.

However, my rugby was suffering. This was largely due to my not being as serious and committed as I could have been, because of my party attitude, wanting to go out on the town and not put in the hard yards to train. Once, aged 17 and in Grade 11, when I was out on the town at a nightclub in Hatfield, Pretoria, I got a call from my dad. It was probably a Friday night. He asked where I was, and then said these words, which really gave me a wake-up call:

What are you doing? When are you going to start seeing that you are not going to become anything if you carry on doing what your mates are doing? You are not going to become what you are supposed to be!

Obviously he saw the talent I had and was frustrated that I was not making good use of it or giving myself a chance to succeed. I was really taken aback by my dad's words to me, and they struck a chord. After that conversation, I was in no mood to party and went home. Dad, being who he was, with his wealth of experience and talent, obviously knew that wishing to be successful never made anybody a success. Nor would knowing all the ways to be successful make you a success. Here is a statement I like, because it neatly summarises the powerful truth about success that my dad was trying to drill into me:

> Success is neither magical nor mysterious. Success is the natural consequence of consistently applying the basic fundamentals.[9]

What this highlights to me is that the basic fundamentals for success are hard work, discipline and sacrifice. I was deceiving myself into believing that I could achieve all of my goals while carrying on with the ill-disciplined lifestyle I had at the time. There is no getting around it: if you want to achieve your goals, then the principles of hard work, discipline and sacrifice must be observed. That phone call from my dad set me down the right path and back to the plan that I had for my life.

CHAPTER 3

Training: The transformation begins

Pain is temporary. It may last a minute, or an hour, or a day, or a year, but eventually it will subside and something else will take its place. If I quit, however, it lasts forever.

Lance Armstrong

After that wake-up call from Dad, I started training seriously and got into a proper training schedule with a conditioning coach, Jannie Brooks, who was a qualified biokineticist. He also played for Northern Transvaal and Bulls, and was a friend of my dad. He was a great guy and ran his own gym. In fact, my family still trains there. Jannie was a phenomenal trainer and I was in good hands. He had a great plan for me and measured my body, taking regular body mass index (BMI) readings, which indicate the proportion of fat percentage to muscle. Jannie was a pure professional, and the training programmes he put together for me were really well structured.

I was on a proper, effective programme to increase my strength and speed. My dad's overall instruction to Jannie was, 'Make him train hard and develop himself to become great!' Within the first month, I gained four kilograms of muscle and my body responded very well to the training: I became stronger and faster.

Those early gym workouts with Jannie began when I was 17 and focused on the following key areas to help me gain speed and strength:

Legs: Squats, leg press, calf raises, one-legged squats and lunges

Core: Strengthening the stomach muscles with pull-ups, crunches

Upper body: Bench press, incline bench, shoulder press, pull-ups and dips

My early gym workout

That was in 2002, and today the boys start even younger. My advice is to start with light weights and under professional supervision and advice. There's a problem I see all too often: when people start out, they want to go straight for the heavy weights, not realising the harm it can do. I started heavy weight training only when I was 17. Under Jannie's supervision I gradually increased my weights, but certainly didn't jump in and go extremely heavy right at the beginning. I had done some weights when I was 16, but those were lighter and specifically for athletics, to help me with the discus. However, I had no proper programme then, and I was not regular at it – and definitely not as committed.

When I was 15 years old I did 50 push-ups daily for 40 days, and my body responded well. Every day, without fail, before I went to bed I completed those push-ups. My physique changed, which confirmed that my body responds very well to training. I attribute this to the genes I inherited from my father – what some call 'fast-twitch fibres' – and a capacity to thrive under training. Let me also stress that you don't become a superstar in the gym; it helps, but it doesn't make you a great rugby player. Superstars are made on the field: it's what you do with what you have. But being in great shape gives you a much better chance to become great and helps prevent injuries. I like what that great former heavyweight boxing champ Muhammad Ali said about this:

> Champions aren't made in the gyms. Champions are made from something they have deep inside them – a desire, a dream, a vision.

When guys look at me and see my physique, they want to hit the gym and train hard. It's good to be strong and fast, but ultimately it's about how you play on the field. When you do weight training, it's important to know that correct form is always the key. It is better to work with a lighter weight and do it correctly than use a heavier weight and do it wrong. I was taught these important principles:

A long muscle is better than a short muscle.
Remember, you are training a movement, not a muscle.

This table shows how my strength increased over the years:

AGE	MAXIMUM BENCHED WEIGHT
17	130 kg
18/19	145 kg
20	150 kg
21	170 kg
26	180 kg

Pierre's progress on maximum bench press

My ideal playing weight is 107 kilograms. I believe that the moment you become too heavy your fitness goes down, and in some cases you can lose your agility and speed. For me, 107 kilograms
gives a good balance of speed and power. Here is a breakdown of my mass gain and increase in shoe size over the years.

AGE	MASS (KG)	SHOE SIZE
13	55	11
14	65	11
15	75	12
16	88	12
17	92	12
18	103	13

Pierre's weight gain and increase in shoe size

Some other stats

My ability to do pull-ups with a 50 kilogram weight between my legs has improved, so now I use an 80 kilogram weight. I can jump from a standstill onto a 1.5-metre-high platform. On a repeated sprint-ability test I can sprint for 835 metres before slowing down, and currently my body fat percentage is 6.5%. My time over 100 metres is still 10.7 seconds, and I believe I can go even faster. But even though these are just fitness stats, they do encourage me to reach certain goals and to stretch the limits of my body.

My dad was very supportive from when I was a little boy, always encouraging us through words of affirmation, letters or just a simple SMS Here are some of the motivational text messages he sent me in 2003:

> 1 October: Blessed are you oh great one in the name of the Lord. His goodness and favour is your path, every place your foot treads has been given to you.

> 1 October: My beloved son, you have sown seeds of discipline and commitment and you are reaping the reward. It's only the beginning, now it is a new level of focus and dedication.

> 16 October: You have entered the bullring of champion leaders, where it is mighty lonely. Everything you do is closely watched by everybody: your clothes, hair, speech, shoes and conduct. The nation is the paparazzi. Leaders live and walk where the eagles fly. You are a great leader.

Dad would also further inspire me to be a great leader with words like these:

> Good leaders get their hands dirty – leading by example and great leadership is all about influence.

> Pierre, your leadership style needs to be encompassing of people you are leading and not just centred around yourself.

Dad also monitored my progress. He would check with Jannie whether I had attended my workout sessions and enquire about how I was doing. He would also call me to check my progress and get my feedback.

The results of my hard work at training were beginning to be seen. After all, I was at the gym up to three days a week (between my rugby and athletics training) and putting everything into it. I was really committed to the training and made sure that I worked hard at it, as I wanted to succeed and attain my goal of playing for the Bulls – and eventually the Springboks.

My training schedule in those early days looked something like this:

5:30am–6:30am: gym, then shower and head to school

2:30pm–4:30pm: rugby and/or athletics training

6pm–8pm or 7pm–9pm: choir practice (twice a week)

My personal timetable in 2003 (matric)

Quest for greatness

In training I believe it's your mind that determines your effort. Most people never give themselves a chance to attempt certain things because they simply believe they cannot achieve them. They are holding themselves back from greatness – whether it's on the field or just getting into good shape.

If I had never attempted those box jumps or pull-ups or suchlike things, I wouldn't be where I am today. (But please don't try anything silly and hurt yourself. Be responsible!) All I am saying is: give yourself a chance and aim high. You will be surprised at what you can achieve.

Whether you think you can or think you can't – you're right![10]

Diet and nutrition

I love eating healthily and I don't eat junk. I strongly believe that 80% of your training success results from what you put into your body. The correct amount of liquid, food, rest and recovery, combined with the right training, will cause your body to respond positively – that's a fact! It's no use training to exhaustion if, on the other hand, you're putting rubbish into your body. It doesn't make sense. It's like lovingly washing the exterior of your car, then pouring all that dirty, soapy water into the fuel tank.

Because I'm physically very active and have a fast metabolism, I can eat a lot. Just ask my wife: she's the one responsible for feeding me when I get home in the evening! Even with my big appetite, especially after a workout, I'm very careful about what I eat. Generally in the mornings I'll have some Weet-Bix or oats with fruit, a scoop of peanut butter and my multivitamins, and then go off to gym to start at 9am. I have a light breakfast because it isn't wise to train on a big meal. I also make sure that I'm hydrated: I usually have an energy drink (non-fizzy) before and during training, as well as lots of water.

Within an hour after gym training, I usually get into some brunch or make sure I get some kind of recovery supplement like Pure Protein or BCAA. Nothing fatty, or with skins – eggs, toast and sausages. At Loftus we have a great restaurant with wonderful service and food. For brunch I usually have the following:

- chicken without skin
- vegetables and salad
- pizza maybe once a week
- eggs, sausages, bacon (no fat)
- toast

For the evening meal I generally have more protein than carbs, and when I'm at home my wife makes us a nice dinner. For just the two of us she makes dinner for four: as I mentioned, I have a big appetite! But again, it's all healthy:

- beef, chicken, fish, steak
- starch: couscous, mealies, potatoes (no butter), sweet potatoes
- steamed vegetables

A nice snack for me is yoghurt and muesli or breakfast cereal. I am not a big fan of dessert, but do have it on some nights. I like dark chocolate especially, and chocolate with nuts. If you ever have me around to your house, make sure you serve my favourite dessert, which is malva pudding. If you're South African, you will know all about malva pudding. For the benefit of those who aren't, it's a sweet pudding of Dutch origin made with apricot jam, and has a spongy caramelised texture. It's usually served hot with either custard or ice cream.

Now the proviso about this dessert: you have to earn it. By this I mean you need to have done an intense workout or a long run before enjoying this dessert, otherwise it will defeat the purpose of training so hard. Note that I don't have malva pudding every day – probably just once a month. I guess when it comes to eating healthily, you have to create a good balance and be aware of what goes into your body, even the finer details. But I have learnt not to be painfully picky of what I eat – believe me I sometimes lose it and have way more than I should, but then I just make sure I cut back again on other days or meals.

Usually after dinner I enjoy a good cup of coffee to end my day. Juanné bought me a coffee machine for my birthday, so that we don't have to go out for really good coffee. Again, like dessert, too much coffee isn't good for you. Also remember that alcohol and smoking limit your body's ability to perform. Don't think you can drink and smoke and still expect to perform at your best. These habits are a huge extra burden, and one that is totally unnecessary, because you can choose to avoid them.

Back to my journey. I was training hard and at an exciting point, because I could see the results and expected good things. I knew what was to come was going to be great. My sister Johanni, on the other hand, had fallen pregnant, so she was at a place of pain, doubt and not knowing what to do, and she felt judged. It was quite ironical that we were living in the same house, with her at a low point in her life while I was at the other extreme.

I was 17 years old and coming up to my Grade 11 exams, which were very important because it was those results on which universities decided provisionally whether or not to accept applications for enrolment. At that time, though, our home was in turmoil – financially, personally and emotionally. However, the one thing I had going for me was my success in sports, which was starting to take off. I'll talk about the family's tough times in the next chapter.

I went into 2003 with more confidence, as my body was responding and I was in much better shape than the previous year. It was also my matric year, my final year of schooling, so I wanted to give it my all. And of course we all felt excited at being about to leave school, and that great vibe of now being the seniors and leaders of the school.

Athletics that year started with our interhouse competition. I did really well, coming first in the 100 metres, 110-metre hurdles, shot put and discus. My dad was there and loved it. He was extremely proud and began to see that what he had had in mind for me was starting to fall into place. He shared with me his thoughts on my progress:

> My son was understanding the purpose he was born with – to be the best he can be.

At Affies, like most high schools, the interschool athletics meeting takes place before the rugby season kicks off. The relays are always the main attraction, and it's an Affies tradition for the relay teams to wear full white body suits. Everybody seemed to love the suits, but I can't help wondering whether it wasn't because they emphasised our crotch areas! Our arch rivals were Waterkloof High School, and the competition between the two schools was always tough. At that particular point of the athletics meeting, with just this last relay race to go, I found out that we were already ahead in the combined points tally, and all we needed to guarantee overall victory in the athletics meeting was for me to finish second, as I was anchoring the relay.

Earlier, in the 100-metre sprint, I came a disappointing fourth, as I had stretched incorrectly and for too long before the race. This resulted in me blanking out and fading after leading for the first 50 metres. In the anchor leg of the relay, I knew the guy running against me was quick and was a specialist sprinter, whereas I was a discus thrower who could run fast. He was also at least 20 to 25 kilograms lighter than me – a huge weight advantage for him. As we rounded the last corner I could see him accelerate and begin to pull away from me, leaving me behind. As we finished I could see the Waterkloof students cheering and going crazy, as though they had won the day. But even though we had lost the relay, I had done enough to finish second, which gave us overall victory – although I was denied the opportunity for the traditional victor's celebration, of racing past the other competitors with arms raised and shouts of satisfaction. It wasn't the perfect combination, but we won overall.

All in all, at that time of my life I was producing the results I wanted, and the hard work and training I was enduring made me disciplined in all areas of my life. I loved the choir because I enjoyed singing and a lot of my mates were in the choir. It was a different environment from rugby, as we were a group of about 90, instead of 15, and our only goal was to sing well. I firmly believe that you have to do something with whatever talents you have. I can even play the piano, taught by my sister Johanni, and I learnt a little guitar from my friends. My discus went really well, and I won the SA championships with a throw of 55.28 metres with the 1.75 kilogram discus, which qualified me for the world junior championships. I also came third in the shot put. These achievements were a huge improvement over my last efforts at primary school.

But I was also excelling at my rugby, and so I was confronted with a choice: whether to pursue a professional career in athletics or rugby. In hindsight I'm glad I chose rugby. Wouldn't you agree? Besides rugby, I was blessed with other sporting talents. In my age group, under 20, I was South African number one in discus and number three in shot put.

Was all of this a matter of luck? I don't think so. I strongly believe that if you want to achieve anything in life, then you have to be deliberate about getting it. What do I mean by 'deliberate'? You have to start every day with your goals clearly in mind, and be focused. You can't live as if it's going to fall into your lap. You have to work hard. And it starts in the training, definitely not on game day. You can't expect to be able to turn it on come the day of the game, definitely not. It takes time, preparation and planning. I love what the immensely talented American basketball player, Kobe Bryant, says about this:

> I really don't give it that much thought. A lot of people talk about it, and they say how difficult it is to do. I just go out there and I work hard.

That year in 2003 I captained Affies and we didn't fare well in the *Beeld* Trophy, the prestigious high schools rugby tournament. We lost eight out of 22 games and finished mid-table, missing out on the finals. Despite our disappointing performance I was chosen to captain the Blue Bulls at Craven Week in 2003, and really excited to play well enough to make the SA Schools. We lost to Free State, which was full of Grey College boys.

That year I didn't score at Craven Week, but I scored 16 tries for my school.
More important than the great rugby I experienced at Craven Week
was the special friendship I was able to establish through it with one of my
'opponents', a friendship that has lasted up until today. I have asked that
friend, Joey Mongalo, to share some memories of us at that time.

Joey Mongalo
Friend and Craven Week roommate

'In that very moment I knew there was so much more to this
man than his being just another all-time-great rugby player.'

I first met Pierre at the Blue Bulls Under-16 rugby trials in 2001. I was at
Pretoria Boys' High and he was at Affies, two schools that are traditional
rivals, with just a railway line separating them. It was a healthy rivalry
though: the tenacious but well-mannered English-speaking boys from
Boys' High versus the rough, self-confident, almost arrogant Afrikaans-
speaking Affies *seuns* (boys). To my knowledge Pierre went pretty much
unnoticed through Grades 8 and 9. But he hit quite a growth spurt
in 2001, aged 16, throwing the javelin miles in the athletics season,
running the 100 metres quite briskly for a young man his size, and
carrying the ball rather effectively in the rugby season. So, as you can
imagine, all those stories about him were much exaggerated by the time
they became rumours that crossed the railway line and found their way
to Pretoria Boys' High.

After this first encounter with Pierre, I was pleasantly surprised when
I met him again at the 2002 Craven Week. I had expected a robust,
hardcore Afrikaans-only-speaking teenage giant, but there was much
more to him than that, as I gradually discovered. He had more depth
than the rumours had made of him. He was more than just a potentially
great athlete: he had culture, singing in the Affies choir, and was always
up for a good laugh. Confident, but humble and considerate, he was
open and receptive, a potential friend in the enemy's camp. The two
things that impressed me the most about Pierre have become the base
or foundation of our friendship.

• First, he was always considerate in that he chose to converse with
   me in English, even though my Afrikaans is pretty fluent. So when we
   hung out, you would have a black African boy from Brits with a slight

English accent speaking Afrikaans to a white Afrikaans-speaking boy, who would get his tongue muddled up as he tried to reply in English. We had many good laughs correcting one another in our second languages. The fruits we have since reaped from that exercise have been quite impressive: I got an A for Afrikaans in matric, and Pierre speaks good English in his interviews. So that was an exercise well done!

- Second, Pierre and I spoke and philosophised quite often about girls, life, family, morals, God and Christianity during our last two high-school years, 2002 and 2003, when we were Craven Week roommates. Most people our age shied far away from anything even close to a deep conversation. I think the fact that his mom and dad were divorced, or were going through a tough time, and that I had lost my father when I was young, could have resulted in us seeing a common inner longing for fatherhood in each other's lives. So I believe we discussed and theorised about subjects that other boys our age would learn about from their fathers. This aspect became, and is still today, the foundation on which our friendship is built. Just the other day he joined me for breakfast at my workplace, and we discussed how we could change the world to make it a better place for all of us to live in. I think we both have an inner hunger to guide and lead younger men as the fathers or role models we ourselves do not have, having lost our dads.

Pierre's impact on me

On the field we clicked quite well at the two Craven Weeks we played together, especially the one in Wellington in our matric year, 2003, our second year as roommates. He was one of the most watched and widely spoken-about eighth men at the tournament, so playing at scrum half behind him was rather reassuring: he had a quiet sense of self-confidence and calm that inevitability rubbed off onto me. I appreciated that, because I was always nervous playing at scrum half, as it was my less-preferred position.

I could summarise his on-field impact on me in the following sentence: what more assurance do you need than being led out and playing behind an explosive, almost two-metre, 100-odd-kilogram eighth man? Even though he wasn't always one of those loud-voiced, inspirationally eloquent leaders, he more than made up for it in his character and his play.

Off the field I gained a lifelong – or, even better, eternal – brother. These days we don't get to see each other as much as we would like to, but when we do catch up, it is always easy to pick up just where we left off. I have gained a fellow history maker; we have a major heart to change the world – and, our world being the sports world, that means one person at a time, through example. Pierre keeps reminding me that we were never created to be average, but rather with a major purpose that will touch many lives as we walk in it. He does place a major emphasis on being intentional in life, but also on not taking it all too seriously, as is evident from his Twitter and BlackBerry status updates. 'I came that you may have and enjoy life and have it in abundance, until it overflows.'[11]

Affies vs Pretoria Boys' High 2003: My fame, his failure, love and humility

Every year in June, one of the greatest South African schoolboy derbies takes place in Pretoria: Pretoria Boys' High School versus Afrikaanse Hoër Seunskool, aka Boys' High vs Affies. Pierre, as you know, was born in June, and a win in a derby of this nature would be the perfect cherry on top of his 18th birthday cake – since every rugby-playing schoolboy from either school dreams of representing it in this momentous clash, from the first time they hear about it. Pierre was the captain of the mighty 'Wit Bulle' – a good team on paper, but not on their greatest form – and I was the full back for the 'Candy Stripes' – a team with not much natural rugby talent, but massive character, pride and tradition, captained by Chiliboy Ralepelle, two-times SA Schools hooker and later Springbok.

Pierre, Chili and I were very close now, as we got to see more of each other while training together with the Blue Bulls Craven Week team, but on that particular day we were intense rivals. The hype around the game was always intense, rumours jumping across the railway line between the two schools. And the greatest rumour of all was about the schoolboy legend himself, boy wonder Pierre Spies: 'He is huge, he is exceptionally fast as well, he sings in their choir – is there anything he can't do?' That was just one of the nervous questions being whispered around our school in the days leading up to the match.

Pretoria Boys' High had last won this derby in 1985, the year Pierre and I were born. It was an epic game, with 16 000 spectators. Everything that could have gone wrong for Affies did, and all the 50/50 decisions went our way. The result: we won the match 18–3, and I had the crazy, once-in-a-lifetime privilege of kicking all 18 of our points.

But here is the special moment of that day. After being the first Affies captain to lose to Boys' High in 18 years, this legend of a man walked across to our captain, Chiliboy, and me to congratulate us and be photographed with us. In that moment I knew there was so much more to this man than his being just another all-time-great rugby player. Next to me stood a young man full of grace and humility, with immense character and the ability to be a true lifelong champion on and off the field. His depth was evident at that age already, and I firmly believe that we are yet to see the best of him.

Pierre always used this saying, which reminded us about perseverance and hard work – I think he may have got it from his father: 'Pay now, fly later!' This meant we needed to put in all the hard work now so we could reap the rewards later. He is now certainly enjoying the fruits of the labour that he put in, especially when no one was looking. It is always encouraging to see the successful results of applying a kingdom principle: we all reap what we sow, and from the fruits of Pierre's life, one can't but conclude that much good has been sown.

From Joey's account of his team's victory over mine, you will see that I had improved a lot at being a gracious loser, and had moved on from that golf defeat to my cousin. I am certainly grateful to my dad for teaching this value to me when I was young. As Joey mentioned, my Craven Week performances were being watched closely, and my hard work was soon to be rewarded. My major break in rugby came in 2003, when I was spotted during Craven Week at Wellington in the Cape.

I was playing as a loose forward, at number 8, and caught the eye of the South African Under-19 coach, Eugene Eloff. He was pretty impressed with my speed and power, and said that he wanted to try me out on the wing for the Under-19s. He shared this thought with my dad, who in his time had been a great winger for Northern Transvaal. Dad agreed, as he had always encouraged me to place myself in good positions on the field so that my pace and power could be utilised to the fullest in open play, and putting me out on the wing would serve this purpose very well. In high school I mainly played as a forward, either lock or eighth man. I played wing briefly in 2000, but went back to lock that same year. It was really only after completing my schooling that I would play wing again, in 2004 for the South African Under-19s. Johan van Graan, my coach at Affies from 2002 and now with the Bulls, encouraged me and said I shouldn't worry about it, as it was a minor matter. At the time Johan was also involved in the Junior Bulls structure.

Being spotted at Craven Week was my lucky break, my ticket to the big time, but quite honestly I didn't think that I'd put in a particularly great performance there. Confirmation of this was that I wasn't selected for either the SA Schools or the SA Academy team, which was what you aimed for at Craven Week. Funnily enough, I share this 'failure' with several teammates, the likes of Fourie du Preez, Jaque Fourie, Bryan Habana and Schalk Burger. Even though we didn't play for the SA Schools, we all went on to play for the Springboks by the age of 21.

In my matric year, my final year at school, I received the following awards:

- Ideal Affie – This award was given to the student regarded as providing the best example to the rest of the students. This was given to about six pupils.
- Ambassador's Trophy – An award that required a student to be a good representative of Affies.

I won both of these excellence awards even though at the time I wasn't fully committed to my faith. I was disciplined, however, and I went out of my way to be friendly with people in all walks of life. I just tried to make time for everyone and make people feel welcome in my presence. I had learnt from my dad to lead by example.

When I came to Affies I was small and unpopular. But that just proves that whatever you go through in life, it is not about how you start but how you finish. Don't look down on other people or yourself. Keep looking up and believing in yourself – because your time will come. Remember that even if you don't achieve what you set out to do, it doesn't mean the end of the world. I believe that all things will eventually work out for good!

I can assure you that if you stick to this simple principle, you will go places and achieve great and mighty things. Hold on and keep giving your best. I share this as a lesson I learnt, that in life there may be times when we don't achieve what we set out to achieve, but that's no reason not to persevere.

CHAPTER 4

Tough times

A happy life consists not in the absence, but in the mastery of hardships.

Helen Keller

As things were starting to look up for me at high school, my parents were embroiled in a crisis in their marriage. It was quite evident that my pretty picture of home life was going to change. Over time the communication channels broke down, and when I was 15, in 2000, my parents chose to have a divorce. This was a huge blow to my world and shattered my picture of the family. Even though my parents were having difficulties in their marriage, I am grateful that there was always love in our home, no matter what.

As I said at the outset, I want to be honest and address issues that I feel are truly relevant and important in these times – and one of those issues is the divorce of my parents. As this devastating news sank in, I realised, in my immaturity, that it meant no more family holidays or Christmases together. The security that my sisters and I had gained from being part of a solid family structure as we grew up was now shattered. Satan is a thief, and I believe that he will steal your happiness and joy if you do not look after what God has entrusted to you. The Bible says, in John 10:10, that he comes to kill, steal, rob and destroy, and today he is most certainly after our families through the sanctity of marriage.

I began asking more questions about life, and especially about God:

- How could a loving God allow this to happen?
- Why do bad things have to happen to good people?
- Why do families get separated?

I was young and immature, and only later realised that my parents' divorce was not part of God's plan. God has given us the power of the free will. We often blame God for our decisions, when really they are decisions we have to make ourselves – decisions we will live and die by. I particularly like this verse on the matter of choice:

> I have set before you life and death, blessings and curses. Now choose life, so that you and your children may live.[12]

In life we cannot let the bad decisions our parents make be an excuse to make them ourselves. It's just not good enough to say that because your parents did it, that's why you are doing it. You're better than that! We can certainly learn from the mistakes of others, and that's what I choose to do.

Because the thief's purpose is to kill, steal, rob and destroy, I firmly believe that divorce is one of the weapons that the devil uses to destroy humanity. God has ordained the institution of marriage for this very reason: to cause us to grow up healthy, protected and nurtured. Divorce seeks to destroy this core family unit that God had planned for us. Don't get me wrong: I don't condemn divorce in cases of physical abuse and unfaithfulness. As much as the Bible says that God hates divorce,[13] He doesn't tolerate unfaithfulness, and when partners choose to disrespect each other with physical abuse, that is not honouring God at all.

Sadly the divorce rates today are quite high. Why? Could it be that husbands and wives are not trying hard enough to make their marriages work? Or has it become more acceptable – if a marriage is going through tough times, divorce is seen as the panacea? I am talking about situations when it becomes 'inconvenient' to remain married. Rather than working out their differences, the couple chooses the option of divorce. Study upon study has revealed the devastating effects of divorce on children. It makes children become adults before their time, as they are not emotionally prepared for it. Having experienced the pain of my parents' divorce, I would not wish this on any children, because it is obvious that the people who suffer the most are the children!

The impact of divorce on children

I strongly believe that one of the primary concerns on the breakdown of a married, two-parent family is the impact it has on the innocent children. I say 'innocent' because the children did nothing to deserve the heartache and pain of their parents' divorce. Children do not ask to be born; it's their parents who choose to bring them into the world.

I have read a great deal about the long-term effects of divorce on children and how many of them suffer for years after from social and psychological difficulties associated with the divorce. They also experience heightened anxiety in forming lasting attachments at later stages, including young adulthood. Having been through this terrible situation myself, I can confidently say that it is not part of God's plan for a child – or, for that matter, anyone else – to go through it. It is best for children to be raised by their married mother and father. Studies clearly show that this is the environment in which children are most likely to thrive. Equally revealing are studies of the negative impact when the father-mother structure breaks down, especially in divorce. Before a couple decides to divorce, I would ask them please to consider the future of their children and try to work things out.

Common sense tells us that girls and boys need role models of both genders, but research also reveals that fathers and mothers contribute uniquely to their children:

> The two sexes are different to the core, and each is necessary – culturally and biologically – for the optimal development of a human being.[14]

Let me also clearly state that while the roles of men and women may differ, neither is greater or lesser than the other. I believe that God created us in His image, intentionally male and female, each gender with unique and complementary qualities. The absence of either parent has implications for a child, as was evidenced in mine and my sisters' lives. For example, compared to children from intact homes, children of divorced parents are far more likely to struggle academically, live in poverty, and engage in drug and alcohol use and other high-risk behaviours.

The youngest becoming the eldest

In divorce, children grow up before their time, and that is what happened to me. My family always regarded me as a responsible person, but when my parents divorced, my dad's absence forced me to assume the role of the man in my family. The moment a family is struck by divorce, it goes into survival mode. A marriage is a protected environment, but divorce takes those walls down and exposes you as a child to an unprotected world. You grab hold of whatever you can and hold together as much as you can. But no matter how good an effort you put in to salvage your family, it will never be as good as the initial marriage set-up.

I learnt an important lesson from participating in the relay race in my days at Affies: don't drop the baton! No matter how fast you run, it's wasted if you don't make sure that you hand the baton over safely and securely to your teammate. I recall watching the men's and women's Olympic 4 x 100-metre relay races in the 2008 finals in China, and seeing this hard lesson learnt by both the men's and women's USA relay teams. They were heavily favoured to win, but both dropped the baton during the transfer, and that dashed all hopes of victory.

I believe that life is pretty much like a relay race. Each generation has a responsibility to hand down to the next the 'baton' of good virtues, advice and guidance, to instil in them the important character-building principle of never quitting. Marriage is part of that, and has proved to be the fundamental foundation of any society. My advice to married couples is to cherish their marriage by honouring their vows.

Having experienced, as a child, the hurt that goes with having to endure your parents getting divorced, I can honestly say that it is a painful experience for all family members. Having seen its damage first-hand, I deliberately resolved to make a success of my own marriage. I would learn from my parents' mistakes and avoid them.

My question to parents is: why subject your children to all of this – to the psychiatric problems, relationship failure in adulthood and even suicidal tendencies that are known to afflict children of divorced parents? I understand that people reach a point where they just lose hope.

Things only get tougher at home

After my parents' divorce I chose to live with my mother. I had to assume the role of the man in my mum's and sisters' lives, and there was no way I was going to leave my mum to fend for herself. Things were pretty dire for us financially, and we were barely making ends meet. Steffani was still at home and was sharing a room with Johanni, who was studying through Unisa. My mum, at 42, and having been a stay-at-home mum for most of her life, decided to join Johanni and pursue her lifelong ambition to become a lawyer.

I was proud of my mum for taking the initiative to stretch herself at her age. It was never her goal to become a successful lawyer or businesswoman. She did it to become financially independent and to avoid the victim attitude she could so easily have adopted after the divorce. My sisters and I were proud of her and kept encouraging her in this tough task. I was proud to tell people my mum was studying at her age, as a lot of women who get married young never study. It was tough but she made it through!

I can remember a time when I had to tell friends I'd invited over that they could visit our home, but couldn't stay for dinner! Even then I was able to joke and make the best of it. As much as these were testing times, we never thought we weren't going to make it – Mum just wouldn't allow that! It was actually exciting to plan and work together every month, to see how far we could get with the little we had and we always had a good time together. It's not as if I ever slept hungry: we just didn't have abundance, but there was always enough – always enough! There was always a happy mood in our house, never a negative atmosphere. Always love, excitement and, of course, a healthy dose of positive words. Our attitude was: this is only a phase or a season.

It doesn't rain but it pours

To make matters worse, and right in the middle of our hard financial times, Johanni, who was 23 at the time, and in the final year of her law degree, fell pregnant. The father was her long-time boyfriend. This was another blow to my understanding of life and family. Again my mind was filled with questions:

- How could this happen to a family so committed to serving God?
- What would everyone say?
- How would this look to the outside world?

Johanni's unexpected pregnancy called into question our core moral values. She faced the choice that so many women in her situation face: do I keep the baby? According to the Bible, God knew you even when you were in your mother's womb:

> You made all the delicate, inner parts of my body and knit me together in my mother's womb. Thank you for making me so wonderfully complex! Your workmanship is marvellous – how well I know it. You watched me as I was being formed in utter seclusion, as I was woven together in the dark of the womb.
>
> You saw me before I was born. Every day of my life was recorded in your book.
>
> Every moment was laid out before a single day had passed.[15]

I urge those facing this decision to choose that the baby lives. In our home we were taught that the pain of discipline is better than the pain of regret!

I was really glad that Johanni chose to take responsibility and followed through with her pregnancy. Taking responsibility is the right thing to do, and in the long run it brings forth fruit. Even though it was tough, she held out, and we as her family encouraged her and helped her, with my mum leading the way. It's important to help one another through any tough time as a family. God honoured Johanni for her obedience and blessed her with a beautiful baby girl, Milla. Milla arrived just two weeks before Johanni's final law exam and was a miracle. She came to us at such a difficult time. Today we cannot imagine our lives without this little princess, who is a bundle of life-giving joy!

I understand that couples out of wedlock face a difficult choice when they find that they are pregnant, especially when they are young. They have to contend with societal pressures, and especially with the stigma of, 'What will people think of me, what will they say about me? I've let my family down.' We as a family commend Johanni for making the choice not to abort Milla. I know that this is a tough choice for those involved, and I don't want to come across as judgemental or critical, so I have asked Johanni to give us her personal account of what she went through when she found out that she was pregnant.

Johanni Spies
Abortion or life? The choice is yours

Among my family and friends I had always been regarded as the sensible one, but now I was at the clinic taking a pregnancy test. The result came back positive, confirming my fears. Against my better judgement and all that I had been taught to believe by my parents, I was pregnant – at the age of 23, and unmarried. It happened during the last year of my law degree, by my then long-standing boyfriend. 'What a fool you've been!' I remember telling myself.

My immediate thoughts were of shock and horror. 'Oh no, this can't be happening to me!' Not only had I let my family down, but I could not have picked a worse time to fall pregnant. It didn't fit into my plans, and was pretty inconvenient for my future, or so I thought. And I didn't even like being around children – they irritated me and the thought of having a baby didn't excite me one bit.

I remember thinking that to overcome this 'inconvenience' and disruption of my lifestyle, I could have an abortion. No one would know, and I could merrily continue with my plans for the future. After all, it's not really a baby but a foetus until it's born, isn't it?

I'm so glad I didn't go through with the abortion. Even though I had made a mistake and gone against the values I had been brought up in by sleeping with a guy before we were married, I certainly didn't want to make another mistake by aborting my baby.

I remember approaching my mum in the morning as she was having her toast and tea. I showed her the sonogram image of Milla at six weeks. Mum immediately encouraged me to keep on studying and to stay positive, and assured me that it was going to be OK. She called my dad and I remember him coming over, putting his arms around me and saying, 'Don't worry, my love, everything is going to be OK.'

Many young women find themselves in this situation today, and I can certainly empathise with them. When it hits you, things may not make sense. It may seem dark and as if you are living your worst possible nightmare. But even though it may not make sense at the time, you must understand that there is a God who cares and understands. I also began to blame myself, and became my own worst enemy. You think your life is going to end right there – and you may even contemplate self harm. I felt robbed of my youth, because I'd be stuck at home at only 23, when everybody else was going out and having a good time. I also endured much judgement and criticism from people in our church, especially because my dad and grandparents were regarded as leaders in the church.

Even though my family was shocked at first, they formed an amazing support network around me. We talked openly about my options, and they heard me out without criticising me. Be encouraged by the fact that everything is for a reason. Take heart, what may be unclear now will unfold and reveal itself later. I know this, because what I thought was a burden turned out to be one of the biggest blessings I ever received.

Even though what I had done was not in keeping with my faith, it was my faith that ultimately held me together. Yes, I had done wrong, but the God of the Bible is forgiving, loving and always gracious. People can be judgemental at times, but I was encouraged and heard His words echo in my mind when He addressed the woman caught sinning: 'Let him who has not sinned cast the first stone.'

What had seemed a burden turned out to be one of the greatest blessings in my life when my daughter, Milla, was born two weeks before I wrote my final law exam. Now, eight years later, when I look back, I am so glad that I chose to give Milla life. God took something

From top left: Being serious while watching Mom hanging out the washing.

Me, at age two, in my favourite top: I'm the man of the house!

Early days in the Spies family: Dad, Mom, Johanni, Steffani and 'Ouboet'.

On one of our beach holidays – me and my dad.

From top left: My Grade 1 photo.

Dad in full flight over the hurdles.

Proud primary school headboy.

Me, Dad and Uncle Erwee in one of our shared interests, a Land Rover!

Taking on the rapids on the Swaziland border.

ke father like son. Dad
oring for Northern Province
d me on the run for Affies.

Proud sporting moments at school with my dad after I was named man of the match in our U/16 final against Zwartkop. Dad loved hugging me and bragging about me (sometimes too much!).

Leading our first team out a[g] Maritzburg College.

Thanking the Lord after an U/15 match for the great game we had had.

Taking the baton home for Affies U/17 relay.   Playing some tunes on the piano at home.

With two of my great mates: Chiliboy Ralepelle and Joey Mongalo
after our loss against Pretoria Boys High School.

From top left:

On the farm at Mabula during my first year of varsity. I've let the hair go!

After I broke my arm in our U/19 World Cup.

At home with some mates.

Milla and her Uncle Pierre. My sister Johanni's child has blessed our lives immensely.

Steffani, Johanni, me and Mom at home.

Me and my better half Juanné, putting on our dancing shoes at friend and fellow player Werner Kruger's wedding.

On our honeymoon in the Bazaruto islands off the coast of Mozambique.

On our wedding day, 2 December 2008.

that had seemed harmful to me and turned it around for my own good. In fact, Milla helped get me on the journey back to God, and I became more focused, more purpose-driven. I completed my law degree, and my admission and conveyancing exams before some of my (babyless) friends, as Milla's birth made me more motivated to succeed.

My mum was also in the final year of her law degree, and we would exchange babysitting duties as we juggled around our exams. You can imagine the pressure we were under: having a baby is a major shock to the system. Even Pierre used to help out whenever he could. He and his friends would take Milla to the mall to attract girls as what he called a 'babe magnet'. This was until she needed a nappy change, at which point he'd call me, saying, 'Come on now, this one's too bad.'

Remember that God is the giver of life and doesn't make mistakes. Even though things may not be part of your plan, God is in control. While it may not be your time when things are dark, hold on and don't give up, as your time is coming. I love these words, which encouraged me and reminded me of that very fact:

> I have seen something else under the sun: The race is not to the swift or the battle to the strong, nor does food come to the wise or wealth to the brilliant or favour to the learned; but time and chance happen to them all.[16]

I appreciate that it wasn't easy for Johanni to bare her soul in this way, and I applaud her. Why did she do this? To help others faced with the same choice that she was faced with, and hopefully influence them positively, to choose life. Life is a gift, and as such it should be valued and treasured.

I can honestly say that Johanni's choice to give birth to Milla has brought us untold joy and happiness, and as Milla's uncle I am truly blessed and grateful to have her around. As I write, she is eight years old and an amazing child – talented, beautiful and full of love.

My thoughts

- If you have parents that are constantly arguing and fighting, pray for them, and don't ever blame yourself for their bickering.
- If you are going through tough times in your marriage, before you

consider divorce, go for counselling and try to work through things.

- The trauma and stress inflicted on children when their parents divorce is really high – so parents, please, for the sake of your children, choose to work through your problems and keep the marriage intact.
- As a couple, cherish your relationship from the start, prioritise each other and don't let life become too busy for both of you. If you keep it special, you'll outlast anything!

CHAPTER 5

Good break to bad break

The only disability in life is a bad attitude.

Scott Hamilton

With all the turbulence that I was experiencing on the family front, the one good thing I still had going for me was my rugby. It was slowly but surely starting to take off again. Despite what I thought was a sub-par performance in the 2003 Craven Week, there was a lot still in store for me. After high school I was offered my first professional contract with the Blue Bulls, which I duly accepted and excitedly signed. I was also given a full scholarship to study for a degree in construction management at the University of Pretoria. This was truly an awesome time for me, as it allowed me to experience financial independence and freedom – or so I thought at the time.

After leaving school I moved out of my mum's home and into my own place at the High Performance Centre (HPC) at the University of Pretoria. My life was now my own, to live all alone and away from my family – and I had my own car! That first car of mine was a classic, a 1976 Land Rover Series II station wagon. An old school 'Passion Wagon'! but during that period I only made time for my dad when I needed more money. That was because my first contract with the Bulls was really small in comparison to some of the other players staying with me at the HPC: some earned three times what I did. This was my main reason for always needing extra cash and usually being more or less broke. Hey, but show me a student who doesn't need extra cash? Despite my not making the time for him, my dad still tried to reach out to me.

South African Under-19s

In November 2003 I headed for the South Africa Under-19 trials in Saldhana, and there was a rumour going around that the regime would be similar to the notorious Kamp Staaldraad[17] that the Springboks had been subjected to before the 2003 World Cup. When we got there, we got out of the bus and we had to start running and singing, and realised this camp was not going to be as bad as we had thought. As one of the training exercises, we went out to sea on a boat and were thrown overboard with our lifejackets – at night. We couldn't see a thing and had to get back to shore. Honestly, I enjoyed it even though I felt close to death! I know some people would have been worried about sharks, but I wasn't. Nowadays, those worries only occur in the Currie Cup and Super Rugby competition.

I was selected for the South African squad to play in the upcoming Under-19 World Cup, which was being hosted in South Africa. This was another good break for me that immediately attracted the media spotlight. By then the media had taken note of me and liked the way I played. Having a big physique and playing on the wing, I was even being talked about as the 'new Jonah Lomu' and the 'next big thing' in South African rugby. It was a time when I began to experience the honour of man and rode the 'wave of self-glory'. Being so young, I lapped it all up, but I was soon to find out how temporary it all was, and come tumbling down off this wave.

The unexpected, and tragic, happened to me at that Under-19 Rugby World Cup in 2004, in our quarter-final match against France, when in open play, while carrying the ball up, I was tackled. But it wasn't the tackle that did for me. As I fell to the ground I braced myself by placing my right arm on the ground, and one of the opposition players came crashing in and fell over it, snapping it. Literally a bad break – both bones snapped through!

At the time, as I writhed in pain, I didn't need a doctor to diagnose my injury as a break; it was pretty obvious from the damage and the excruciating pain. On reflection, I realise how quickly it had all happened: one moment I was riding the crest of the wave, and the next moment I was tumbling down. Through this bad break, I was going to learn a valuable lesson, at a very early age, on the fickleness of fame and success.

At first we didn't think the damage was as bad as it eventually turned out to be. We thought that the injury would keep me sidelined for three to four months at the most. If only that had been true!

When the medical team reported that I had badly broken my right radius and ulna, it was a real tragedy for me, as Jake White, the newly appointed Springbok coach, was known to be interested in me. Now I was out for at least three or four months – or at least that's what I was initially told, but there was worse to come. Once again my mind was filled with so many questions, because this was supposed to be my time to reap the rewards for all the effort, investment and sacrifice I had made: Why me, Lord? Why now?

My grandmother explained to me, in her wisdom, that I would only fully understand the relevance of this 'bad break' later. She brought it into perspective: despite my tragic circumstances, God always had a plan for everything, and ultimately it was going to work out for my good. She then further encouraged me by giving me this Bible verse:

> Jesus replied, 'You do not realize now what I am doing, but later you will understand.'[18]

Immediately after the accident, as all my hopes were crashing down about me, I really couldn't make a lot of sense out of what Grandma was trying to tell me. I accepted that she meant well with her advice, but I thought to myself, 'Really, Grandma, what good can come out of this?' I had reached a point where I'd had enough of all of this 'God stuff' that I'd been brought up on. What good was it doing for me? I had cleaned up my life and started working hard on achieving my goals in rugby, and where had that got me?

The break was so severe that two metal plates had to be inserted, as well as 16 screws, eight each to hold my ulna and radius together. It took much longer to heal than the three to four months we originally expected. This was because I didn't take as much care of it as I should have, and largely due to the arm not being in a cast, which was probably more the doctors' fault than mine.

However, I'm not in the blame game, and I'm not pointing fingers or accusing anyone. But in the end the injury took almost a year to heal. A major reason for this long recovery period was a complication in bone development. In the absence of a cast, the bones weren't adequately protected, leading to one of the bones not growing as it was supposed to. I had to be operated on again, including a bone transplant, which required a piece of bone to be removed from my hip and grafted onto my arm. This time the procedure was a success, and, having been injured in April 2004, I would be back playing my beloved rugby in February 2005.

I have to admit that at the time, at 19, it didn't make much sense at all. 'What good can possibly come out of this?' I thought. My arm hadn't healed in the expected time, and I'd been sidelined for ten months. My good old dad still kept on trying to motivate me by saying that I had to remain positive and 'the best is yet to come'.

Yeah, right, I thought to myself, here we go again. I had received this advice earlier from Grandma and here was Dad at it again. I began to doubt this favourite maxim even more after the injury. I was pretty frustrated at this outcome, as I had worked really hard to get as far as I had in the SA Under-19s, and for this to happen was so unfair.

The rebellion

Living on my own at the HPC as a Junior Bulls contracted player, but not being able to train, led to me losing my way. Looking back, I have to acknowledge that this ten-month period was one of the most painful and trying times I have ever been through. I say 'one of' because, little though I knew it, more trying times were to come my way. Because I was not able to play the sport that I loved so much, I began to turn away from the good values and morals that my parents had instilled in me.

Being in the last year of my teens, I was susceptible to peer pressure and getting into the kind of mischief that people my age are noted for. It was not long before I was back into late-night partying, nightclubbing and drinking – slowly but surely slipping away from the things of God. Come to think of it, I did visit church now and then, but for the wrong reasons: I just needed to tick that particular box and, while I was at it, chat up the girls. I may have been in church physically, but I wasn't there in spirit. I did not feel motivated to seek after God, as I had before.

Thanks to my injury, I had plenty of free time on my hands. In theory, this was a great opportunity for me to commit myself to my studies. In fact, I did the exact opposite and began skipping classes. Soon the only thing I was able to pass at university was a rugby ball. Mind you, at that stage, with my injured right arm, I could barely do even that. All that free time turned out to be the perfect excuse for a party. There were three other Junior Bulls players there who were also injured, and together we would plan our parties for weekends and weeknights. We didn't care, as we had enough time on our hands – or so we thought.

I started hanging out at all the nightclubs. I drank lots of alcohol and slowly lost the focus that had previously driven me to succeed. I was in a very bad space. Instead of seeking God in all of my pain, I made the mistake of seeking consolation from my friends. The tragedy was that this led to me being adversely influenced by them. I was seeking acceptance from them, seeking their acknowledgement, and in the process trying to be someone that I was not. I threw myself into a lifestyle of self-centredness: it was all about me.

This is a very bad situation to be in when the focus is on you. There's an interesting fact about 'sin' and 'pride' that I would like to share with you. What do the two words have in common? Think about it. It's the letter 'I', which is at the centre of both words. At the root of sin is selfishness and a focus on the self. I shudder when I think about the things I did back then, and I realise how stupid I was. That's what happens when you get drunk, and I'm thankful to God that even though I was far away from Him, He was still able to keep me from doing serious harm to myself or anyone else.

My relationship with my family, God, going to church, praying and reading my Bible was the last thing on my mind. I was so absorbed with myself and so sorry for poor old me that I didn't realise the harm and damage I was inflicting on myself and my family. My close relationship with my dad was no longer the feature it used to be in my life, and generally setting time aside for God and my family was not at the top of my list. Even though Dad would reach out to me, I didn't make the effort to spend time with him as we did before. I was soon to regret this stupid decision of mine to stay away from the man to whom I owed so much.

The pressure from my peers caused the void in my soul to widen, and I became emptier and emptier. I developed some bad habits thanks to the company I chose to keep. No matter what we may believe, we cannot get away from this truth:

Bad company corrupts good character.[19]

Approaching the end of 2004, I was a wreck spiritually. I had no goals and no motivation to achieve anything worthwhile, and was totally unfocused. I could have successfully completed my first year of studies, but I was too embroiled in my new-found undisciplined lifestyle of loose living. This was all largely due to my 'bad break', my arm taking so long to heal and having to undergo another operation in October. This meant more time away from rugby and had me thinking that things could not get any worse – but I was soon to find out how wrong I was!

I got the message from Dad's brother, my Uncle Dawie, that my dad had been admitted to hospital. Travelling from Johannesburg to Pretoria, he stopped for petrol at a filling station in Midrand, where he was found slumped over the steering wheel. The service station attendant immediately summoned the paramedics, and Dad was taken to hospital.

Around the hospital bed

When we arrived around his bedside, he had an oxygen mask over his face to help with his breathing, preventing him from talking. He was conscious but not able to talk to us – which was a good thing, as, knowing Dad, he would probably have exhausted his precious energy by talking. I remember that he began to cry when he saw us around his bed. It was a very special moment with us all there, even if was only for a few minutes. For once, after the divorce, we were reunited in peaceful circumstances. We all felt something special in the air, and that there was a spirit of reconciliation taking hold right there between Dad and Mum.

We were glad to see it, and it almost gave us a glimpse of a promise of better things to come between them. As their children we were glad of this opportunity for our parents to reconcile. I recall Mum leaning over and kissing his forehead. At that stage it was as if a hold over our family had been broken, presenting us with a divine moment. We all sensed the presence of God in that hospital room around my dad's bedside, and a spirit of reconciliation prevailed over us as a family.

But did my dad listen to the doctor's advice to rest and take it easy and slow down? Oh no, not him. The next morning he got onto a plane and went to George for a motivational speaking engagement. As a self-employed person, Dad was heavily committed financially. He had to work or else he would not get any income, and that was what, I believe, forced him out of that hospital bed and eventually drove him to his grave. It is really sad when you are under so much financial pressure that it takes your life away from you.

My Uncle Dawie sensed how seriously my dad needed to rest, and pleaded with him not to board the plane. He warned him that if he did, we would be holding his funeral in a week's time. Dad, being the kind of man he was, would not heed Uncle Dawie's advice. He went to George, and when he returned on Sunday, he went straight to his home at the Mabula Game Reserve. On Monday morning one of the game rangers found him dead on the porch, slumped over his chair. He had died on Sunday.

The tragedy of my dad passing away

It was a worse blow than not being able to play rugby for ten months. My hero, my idol, my mentor, my dad and my best friend, Pierre Spies Snr, passed away on 31 October 2004. That day will be forever etched in my mind. My mum called me in the morning, at around 7am, to say that I needed to come quickly as she had something urgent to tell us. My sisters and I arrived around the same time. When we had gathered around, she sadly informed us that our father had died of a massive heart attack the previous night.

I thought, how can this be? Dad was only 53 years old and not unfit! My sisters began to cry on hearing the tragic news that our father was no longer going to be around for us. Strangely I didn't cry, as somehow I was prepared. I guess it had something to do with my parents having been divorced for four years. But still the shock for me was huge: you can imagine how devastated I was, being only 19.

I had started 2004 on the crest of a wave. Now I was at rock bottom, with my whole world having rapidly disintegrated beneath me. I admit that I should have made the effort to spend more time with my dad, as we hadn't seen each other much after I moved into the HPC.

My dad's passing taught me some important lessons. One was to give people flowers when they are alive, because it's no use waiting until they're dead. Don't get me wrong, it's nice to present a grieving family with flowers, but what use are the colours and the aroma to the deceased?

This point is nicely conveyed by former All Black Inga 'The Winger' Tuigamala,[20] who became a funeral director after retiring from rugby. In his new profession, he sees the reality and suddenness of death regularly, and challenges people with these words:

> The trouble with most of us is that we are too busy being occupied in things that are not that important. We are imbued with the busyness of this world and it is our relationships with our loved ones that suffer.
>
> I am really amazed at the wonderful floral arrangements that adorn the coffins or gravesides that I have come to frequent through my current business. I am not at all opposed to them as I have seen the comfort that these beautiful flowers can bring to the grieving family and friends in their tribute to their dearly beloved. I often think to myself how much better it would have been and appreciated if these flowers would have been given to the deceased whilst they were alive.

Inga goes on to pose another challenge:

It is good to give flowers to people when they die, but how much better it is to give it to them while they are alive so that they can appreciate it. When last have you given your wife a bouquet of flowers? When last have you treated your loved one to something special? Don't leave it to tomorrow for it may never come and it may just be too late. Common words that I hear at funerals are 'if only'. If only I had done this or that, things would have turned out different. Remember we are on planet earth for a brief time so live your life with no regrets … Why wait to be on your deathbed when you can enjoy being around your family now? Don't be a fool and leave it too late. Maybe there are some changes you need to start making and my advice for you is to start now. Don't put it off any longer before it becomes too late.

I agree wholeheartedly. I faced that hard, cold reality first-hand, losing my dad so suddenly and unexpectedly. Death often comes unexpectedly. The reality we face is that we have to die; we all have to go there some time. Human nature is such that we try to avoid the issue of death at all costs and act like an ostrich with its head buried in the sand. While there are many uncertainties in life, death is a certainty.

Dad, always busy with his work commitments, and I, with my own selfish ways, never made time for each other towards the end. We all have our work commitments, and other things that compete for our attention, but let's face it, how many people do you know who, on their deathbeds, have wished that they'd spent more time at their office, or have asked for their iPhones, BlackBerrys or laptops to give them solace? It's their loved ones, their families, that they want around them as they face death.

There was nothing I could do to bring Dad back, but I could honour his memory by living a life that would have pleased him. As Dad had given me a wake-up call previously when I had strayed, through his death he had given me another reminder.

The Lion King

My dad always referred to himself as the 'Great Lion' and to me as the 'Little Lion'. So Disney's *The Lion King* was a huge hit with our family, as if it was our special movie. You might know that it has a strong father-son theme, and Dad always referred to it when he was encouraging me to take after him and follow in his footsteps, just as Simba did with his father, Mufasa.

In the movie, when Mufasa dies, Simba forsakes his right to his father's throne and goes to live with a wild pig Pumba and a meerkat called Timon. He begins acting and behaving like them, and nothing like the majestic lion, the 'king of the jungle', that he was made to be. He even resorts to eating bugs! The turning point for Simba comes when he goes to the water hole and, looking into the water, sees his image reflected in it. As he looks more closely, he notices his stunning resemblance to his father. As the saying goes, 'Like father like son.' He is then reminded of his father's words to him: 'Remember who you are!' He comes to his senses and immediately sets out to regain his father's throne, which rightfully belongs to him.

I was a type of 'Simba'. I had forsaken the path that my dad had set out for me to walk on for an infinitely inferior lifestyle. Hearing those words, 'Remember who you are!' reminded me of the greatness my dad had predicted for my life.

Dad's passing was my turning point. I couldn't carry on the way I was living. I had taken over some of his roles after the divorce, like looking after my mum and sisters and being the man in their lives. As I mentioned earlier, even though I was the youngest, I became, in a sense, the 'eldest' when my parents divorced, and when my dad died I took on even more responsibilities. I had even bigger shoes to fill.

There is so much more I want to share about my dad that I've allocated the whole of the next chapter to him and our times together.

CHAPTER 6

The Big Lion

A father is a fellow who has replaced the currency in his wallet with snapshots of his kids.

Unknown

It is said that a dad is 'a son's first hero and a daughter's first love'. Of no one is that truer than of my dad. My sisters and I were really blessed to have him as a father. Of course my dad was not perfect; who is? The first thing I want so say is that he was not above reproach, nor was he a saint. Yes, he had shortcomings, but that's not how I want him to be remembered. I loved my father and we had a great relationship. When I was growing up, and I compared him with other kids' dads; I knew that he was special, which meant that I was also special through having him as my father. If had to describe him in one word, that word would be 'unique'.

He was athletic – quick, strong and good at most sports – a poet, and musically talented as a singer, composer, and artist. He had a high IQ, which means he was a quick thinker and someone whom others came to for advice. He was a real genius in many respects.

My dad was a late starter, and his tremendous sporting talent was only realised quite late in his life. He never played first team rugby at school because he was not considered good enough. Nobody believed in him back then, and he was not in any gym or training programme. He was what they call a 'natural'. When he was about 25, he caught the eye of a Pretoria rugby coach when he was playing a game of social rugby at a local park. What alerted this coach was the fact that Dad scored seven tries. It was purely by chance that he was spotted. The coach told Dad that he saw in him a rugby superstar in the making. The next week the coach had Dad in his team, where he scored four tries in his debut. He was immediately promoted into the second team and eventually into the club's First 15. Not long after that, he was gracing the pitch at Loftus Versfeld, wearing the number 14 jersey for Northern Transvaal, the Bulls.

All of this happened in the space of six months – from playing rugby in the park to playing for the Northern Transvaal Bulls. I believe the coach at the time was Buurman van Zyl, one of the most successful Currie Cup coaches of all time, who coached the team to many Currie Cup victories.

Let's not forget my dad's talent as an athlete. He was South African and African record-holder for the 110-metre hurdles and won the prestigious position of being recognised as one of the top five rugby players of the year in South Africa. Being coached by two of the country's top coaches in their respective fields allowed my dad to really excel.

Buurman van Zyl was a former police brigadier and John Short had been an army major. Together they took hold of my dad and began to instil discipline into his life, and within two years, in the 1972/73 season, he became a superstar. In 1975 my dad was at the peak of his career as a Springbok athlete, holding the Africa record in the 110m-hurdles, and also scoring what was regarded as one of the most famous winning tries in South African rugby history, which gave the Northern Transvaal Bulls victory in that historic 1975 Currie Cup final against Free State.

When I was a small boy, people would tell me about that great try, scored in Bloemfontein, in wet, muddy conditions right in the corner. Even today I am approached by people who remember it. I think I might have met every person who was on the stands that day. That performance made my dad a real legend in South Africa. In fact, there's a video of the greatest tries in South African rugby that opens with that very try. It was spectacular, and scored in the dying moments of the game.

1975 Currie Cup final

The 1975 Currie Cup final gave Free State home ground advantage, presenting them with one of their best chances to win. The scores were level at 6–6, and they thought that holding on to a draw was good enough. Everyone thought the game was over, but the Northern Transvaal Bulls had a line-out near the halfway line. The field was wet and muddy, as a hailstorm had lashed the area earlier, and it was not in the best possible state, making playing conditions even worse.

The ball went through about two phases, and for some reason came through quickly, out to the backline, and an amazing thing happened. The centre, Christo Wagenaar, kicked the ball forward, which you would never do in the dying seconds of such a crucial game. He should rather have kept it in hand and passed it to the game breaker and match winner, my dad, Pierre Spies Snr, who was right next to him. Dad was in hot pursuit, and as the ball bounced about in those wet, muddy conditions, by some miracle it bounced up with my 6-foot 5-inch father, an athlete capable of 100 metres in 10.4 seconds, charging at it. He encountered the ball at flat-out speed, and it wobbled on the tips of his fingers. The crowd held its breath.

Slippery as the ball was, he somehow held on to it and scored in the corner. As this was the first-ever televised Currie Cup final, the try was seen by the majority of rugby fans in the country. It was also shown over and over again because it was such a great try. The commentator described how devastated the Free Staters looked, because my dad had robbed them.

The then president of South African Rugby, Danie Craven, missed this great try altogether. He thought that the game was over and began walking down from his seat to present the trophy. He missed what was regarded as the best try of the century. All the photographers also missed the try, except the photographer from *Beeld*, who managed to snap three pictures of my dad scoring.

You'd think, if you listened to me relate this famous try of my dad's, that I had been there. I have seen it many times on video and have had it told to me by Dad and many other people. But by the time I was born, Dad had retired from all forms of competitive sport, so my own memories of him are far away from the rugby field and athletics track.

My dad made trophies for all of us kids. Because he called himself the 'Big Lion', on my trophy he engraved 'the best little lion in the world'. On Johanni's trophy he engraved 'the best eldest sister in the world', and lastly, for my sister Steffani, whom he affectionately called his 'round head', he engraved 'the best little round head in the world'.

As children we were so proud of those trophies and we carried them with great pride. Even now, as I remember that time, I can still sense the great pride that trophy from my dad instilled in me. It's something that I will do with my kids for sure, because as a child you are looking for that affirmation and always seeking approval. How great for children to receive that from their own home instead of seeking it outside! Could that be why children are getting into all kinds of trouble today, when the situation at home is not right?

My dad was never embarrassed about his children, and everywhere he went he used to speak very proudly of us. We were the ones who used to get embarrassed because of all the compliments he would pay to us in public. But that's how my dad was: he was never afraid to show his love, affection, appreciation and approval for and of us. At that time, this was not the norm in our culture.

I recall a time when he taught this quality at one of his men's camps in Mabula. I was outside playing with the other kids when he called me to come inside and join him on stage. In front of about 250 men he did something that at the time that was regarded as strange and, according to my Uncle Dawie, 'changed and started a new legacy in South Africa'. My dad called it 'speaking blessings and life' into someone.

My dad was an astute Bible scholar and had a very good command of the Scriptures; hence he followed the example of the Jewish fathers in the Old Testament, who used to speak favour and God's blessings over their children. I admit that at the time I was annoyed at being interrupted while playing with my friends, and also very uncomfortable and shy at having to stand in front of those 250 men. I was only about eight years old. When I was up on the stage alongside him, he turned to the men and said, 'Today I am going to show you something very special and explain to you a reality that you may not have been aware of.'

Then he placed his hands on me and began speaking positive affirmation and blessings over me:

Pierre, my son, today I am going to deliver a message from God to you. As you are my son I am going to show God's legacy that works through Jesus Christ, His own Son, and from Abraham. These men will see and realise that God is faithful to His word. As your father I want to bless you. I speak into your life the blessings of Deuteronomy Chapter 28. Surely goodness and mercy shall follow you all the days of your life and all that you do will be blessed …

My dad continued in this vein for about ten minutes, and I stood there without much idea of what was going on. I remember asking him, 'Can I go now?' and his replying, 'No, not yet, I haven't finished.' Then he turned to the men and said something on the lines of, 'Please observe very carefully what I am going to do next.' My Uncle Dawie, who was present that day, said that what they witnessed next was something even more special, and challenging to the core of our culture.

My dad put his arms around me and hugged me and kissed me. This, according to Dawie, was something that Afrikaner dads were not used to doing. Most dads were not at ease with hugging their sons, let alone kissing them – they probably didn't know that it was OK for fathers to do this. He explained to me that generally back in that era, men didn't have a very open relationship with their children. The philosophy that many fathers subscribed to was, 'Children should be seen, not heard.' Having a boy being invited into the domain of the men's territory was certainly not the norm.

My dad was seen as violating protocol, firstly by calling me into the meeting, and then by going as far as hugging and kissing me. I believe that my dad could sincerely do that because he personally knew the 'Father heart of God', because of his personal relationship with His Son, Jesus Christ. That day my dad broke with tradition and started something new.

Dawie saw this from the back of the hall and thought it was not very 'South African' of my dad to be doing all of this blessing and hugging stuff. After the meeting Dawie confronted my dad on what he had just done, and tried to call him to order. 'What you are doing is not the way we were brought up. It's just not the right thing and certainly not in keeping with the our culture and tradition.'

My dad replied, 'My brother, I don't care about your feelings and your traditions. I have been tasked by God to fulfil what He says in the Bible.'

He was referring to this Scripture:

And he will turn the hearts of the fathers to the children,
and the hearts of the children to their fathers,
lest I come and strike the earth with a curse.[21]

Dawie still was not convinced, and said, 'This boy is going to get a swollen head if you keep on telling him that he is special and blessed.'

Dad again replied, 'My brother, you watch this boy, this son of mine. Today I spoke his destiny into being according to faith by God's Word. You will see that no teacher, friend or negative opinion will ever prevent God from fulfilling the words of his father spoken over him today. Nothing will influence him, because I am his father. According to the authority that God has given me, I have proclaimed blessing and a bright future for his life. Stop seeing the physical in this, because it is a spiritual thing, which cannot be comprehended or understood by your human mind. Mark my words: you will see that what I have spoken today will come to pass over him according to Proverbs 18:21: "Death and life are in the power of the tongue, and those who love it will eat its fruit."[22]

Over the years my dad's example rubbed off on my Uncle Dawie, and today he shares my dad's passion for teaching about the Father's heart with all people. Let's hear directly from him.

Dawie Spies
My uncle

I may be biased because he was my brother, but I have never in my life seen anybody as talented as my brother Pierre Spies Snr. In my eyes he was a complete and an extraordinary man. John Short, who was one of the best athletics coaches in South Africa, said that he was the most talented specimen he had ever seen, because he excelled at high jump, long jump, hurdles and triple jump. Whatever my brother attempted, he succeeded in. We were always in the shadow of this great man, who I was so proud to have as a big brother.

The camps that he organised and ran were the first men's camps of their type, and they started in the Northern Transvaal, later the Northern Province of South Africa and now Limpopo, at a place called

Mabula. In those old apartheid days, most of the Afrikaner people were very religious and conservative. Their minds were not open to change, and they were hardened in their thinking. Pierre Snr was quite a revolutionary in his thinking, in the way he got the guys out of their comfort zones and spoke about basic realities of life and how to be a 'king, priest and prophet' according to the Bible and truly a man of God. He enjoyed teaching and explaining about the Father's heart. By the camps he ran and his ministry through sports, he started to break up the old and forge ahead with new things, and he really challenged people's thinking about who God was to them. Over the ten years he ran the camps, I would say at least 60 000 people visited them.

Today I can see my brother's influence over the whole country of South Africa living on – not just through his son, but I believe that he prepared the way for the men's camps we have today. Long before Brother Angus Buchan started the Mighty Men camps, he broke the barriers of the Christian mindset to prepare the turning of the hearts of the fathers to their children and the children back to the fathers. This was certainly not the normal thing among us men back then.

My brother was very knowledgeable about the Bible, and knew when he heard from God, so I am glad that he never backed down from what I thought, at the time, was his 'radical thinking'. We grew up in a family of five brothers and one sister, with my brother Pierre the eldest. He was really and truly our role model and the example we followed and looked up to. When we got together as adults, he always bragged about his son, Pierre – so much so that it began to annoy us, because he made such a fuss about Pierre that we didn't get the opportunity to talk about our sons. I remember telling him, 'Please, when we come together, let's not talk about our sons.'

We brothers got together every year for a family tradition that we called a 'five nations' golf competition. (It was at one of those that the ten-year-old Pierre Jnr lost against his cousin and cried.) More important than the golf, we would have a time of praying for each other as brothers and get our sons together as well. It was our Spies 'tribal thing' that Pierre Snr started. We would talk to the boys and mention all the good things they had done and would go on to do in the future. We would also let them know that as their fathers' brothers and their uncles, we would back them up and support them through life. Then all five uncles would speak blessings over their sons and nephews. This was also to reassure them that if anyone was against them, their uncles would be behind them.

I am proud to say that my brother was one of the handful responsible for bringing about change in the mindsets of our people. He achieved this through the organisations he helped found, Sportsmen for Christ and Athletes in Action South Africa, with the support of Neville Norden (South African bodybuilder and Mr South Africa) and Hannes Marais (former Springbok captain). My brother went after these gifted sportsmen and challenged them and said to them that they needed to help bring about change and be witnesses for Christ.

I also remember that my brother was not allowed to speak from the pulpit at the more traditional churches, because our father was a missionary of the Apostolic Faith Mission. He would still get invited, because he was famous, but he was only allowed to speak in the church hall, never from the pulpit of the church itself, which was regarded as too sacred.

My brother had the courage to start something new: he persuaded South African men that it was not only the priests in the churches who knew the Word, and pointed them back to the Bible. This was against the mentality that was drilled into people at the time.

My brother was far ahead of his time, and that's why he was seen by some as radical. His famous words to me were, 'Get into the Word, Dawie.' As the founder of Athletes in Action South Africa, he used his influence as a well-known sports personality to mentor other Christian athletes and sportsmen in South Africa. You just had to sit for five minutes in his presence and you would be captivated by him and see how exceptionally blessed he was. It was these amazing qualities that made such a huge impact on his son Pierre.

My brother was one of the best motivational speakers South Africa ever had. He made three audio CDs, but sadly no videos. He was a flamboyant and articulate speaker who had a remarkable way of opening up people's hearts and no problem holding their attention. He certainly had charisma and charm. And he could be as funny as a comedian.

I have followed in his footsteps and am a speaker as well. As I move around the country, people often remind me that everything my brother told them about his son, Pierre, has indeed come to pass. The people in the Free State joke with me and say they still hate him because he robbed them of Currie Cup glory back in 1975 with that try Pierre Jnr described so accurately a little earlier. I believe that it was one of the most memorable tries in South African history.

The talent we now see emerging in my nephew Pierre, his father saw in its entirety a long time ago, by faith. The young Pierre Jnr, as far as we could see, was a thinker and not a talker like his father – he was very pure in heart. Even now, whenever he speaks, it is always sensible and carefully considered. As he grew we as a family could also see that this boy was very special. I recall my father, Pierre's grandfather, saying to me, 'This Pierre, he has got very, very special abilities, and he is a very special boy.' When I asked him why, and what it was specifically he was referring to in Pierre Jnr, he said, 'I can't quite put my finger on it, but God has a very strong anointing on his life.'

I commend my brother and his wife for raising Pierre in the ways of God. My brother was a fair disciplinarian and always called Pierre back into line when he had to. I also recall that he wrote many letters to motivate Pierre. He went even further and wrote a song especially for Pierre in Afrikaans called 'Ou Boet', which prophetically spoke about Pierre's impact on the fans at Loftus.

Back in the day I thought that Pierre would grow up to be a rowdy boy and proud, but his upbringing didn't allow that. His parents grounded him in humility, and I see that today when I visit his church. Even as a world-famous sportsman, he has not forgotten his roots and who he is. At his church I see him setting out and stacking the chairs, which amazes people. I detect a lot of my brother's influence in Pierre when I see how open and approachable he always is to the younger kids, and how he goes out of his way to put people at their ease. He is never too proud to chat with anyone and always has time for everyone.

He is very respectful to his uncles and always listens to us. He had a tremendous respect for my late mother: as famous as he was, he would sit at her feet and listen to her. Just before her death he went to her, and she blessed him. For me a true sign of his greatness is how, when I am speaking around the country, I hear from people about how they adore Pierre because of his actions. They admire his humility and good manners, and how he manages to keep his cool in the heat of a rugby game. They see him as a very likeable person.

And these compliments are not only from Bulls supporters, but also from supporters of teams that are the Bulls' bitter rivals. That is the true mark of someone with the favour of God upon their life, as the Good Book says, 'When a man's ways please the LORD, he makes even his enemies to be at peace with him.'[23]

Dad, the disciplinarian

Uncle Dawie talked about my dad as a disciplinarian, and that got me thinking about some of the times when he disciplined me. He really taught me to be obedient, which is an area I see so many children struggling with. It all comes down to discipline – and when I say 'discipline', I'm not talking about rigid army-style discipline or abuse. Proverbs says,

> My son, do not despise the chastening of
> the LORD, Nor detest His correction;
> For whom the LORD loves He corrects, Just as a father the son in
> whom he delights.[24]

These Scriptures are further expanded on by the Apostle Paul, who sheds more light on discipline according to the Bible, to show that godly discipline is imposed out of love, not hate or anger,

> As you endure this divine discipline, remember that God is treating you as his own children. Who ever heard of a child who is never disciplined by its father? If God doesn't discipline you as he does all of his children, it means that you are illegitimate and are not really his children at all. Since we respected our earthly fathers who disciplined us, shouldn't we submit even more to the discipline of the Father of our spirits, and live forever?
>
> For our earthly fathers disciplined us for a few years, doing the best they knew how. But God's discipline is always good for us, so that we might share in his holiness. No discipline is enjoyable while it is happening – it's painful! But afterward there will be a peaceful harvest of right living for those who are trained in this way.[25]

When I was little and started walking, my dad warned me not to go near the pool. Being that young, I didn't listen and I fell in. Dad dived in and saved me and that taught me a valuable lesson at a young age: listen to Dad!

One Christmas when I was about ten years old, I got a bow-and-arrow set as a present, and he made it clear that I was not to shoot at people, or even point it at anyone. That summer we went on holiday to Amanzimtoti, on the coast near Durban. I went to the beach with my new bow-and-arrow set and played with it, shooting around. I pointed it at a high-school student who was close by, who came over and told me not to do that again. I didn't listen (as you can see, I was a bad boy too!) and I made as if I was going to shoot at him again, and the boy turned around and slapped me. Right on the cheek – a real burner! I ran straight to my dad, crying, and telling him that this older guy had hit me in the face. Dad was furious seeing his beloved son being bullied by older boys. He ran down to the beach, found the guy and severely reprimanded him demanding a reason for him slapping me.

When things had settled down, the older guy explained to my dad the circumstances that had resulted in him slapping me. Dad turned to me in embarrassment and said, 'Pierre, you go up and wait for me.' I knew what was in store for me, and as I walked back to our beach flat I began to cry. Dad felt really lousy for scolding that boy, and in the beach flat he gave me a hiding for not listening to him and for pointing my arrows at people.

On another occasion I was misbehaving in the car. He told me to be quiet, but I just carried on. Then he said that if he had to remind me again to be quiet, he would buy ice creams for my sisters and not for me. I thought to myself that he would never do that, because he loved me too much, so I went on making a noise. True to his word, when we stopped he bought my sisters an ice cream each and got nothing for me. Being the baby that I was, I started crying as I realised that if I'd listened to him in the first place, I would have got my share of ice cream. I mean – who withholds ice cream from their undisciplined children? But having the heart that he had, and seeing that I was sincerely sorry and had learnt my lesson, he gave me half of his ice cream.

Through these and many other examples, I learnt that every person needs some form of discipline, as it puts a structure around you and brings out the best in you. I am grateful to my dad for his firm discipline, as I believe it has helped shape me to be what I am today. In the game of rugby, if a team is not disciplined, it will be constantly penalised by the referee, who might even award penalties or points to the opposition.

Letters from dad

The problem with many dads is that they struggle to communicate with their children, especially when the kids get older. When they are little, it seems a bit less complicated, but when the kids grow up, sometimes they lose touch with them. My dad always wrote us letters. He may not always have had the best ways of communicating with us kids, but he expressed himself better in letters. Even though he was a good communicator, when he put things onto paper, we could understand more clearly.

My father taught us to always be the best we could be, and he wrote each of us a song when we were little. Mine went something like this:

> My naam is Ouboet en ek is my pa se bul.
> Ek is nog maar baie klein, maar Loftus gaan nog brul
> Al wil ek nooit aan die lag kom nie en almal sê ek is nors,
> Bly ek nog die baas, met 'Big Shot' op my bors.

In English it loses its effect, but here's the English translation anyway:

> My name is Big Brother, and I'm my father's bull.
> I'm still very small, but one day Loftus will roar.
> Though I never want to laugh, and everyone says I'm grumpy,
> I'm still the boss, with 'Big Shot' on my chest .

He had so much faith in me and prophesied that poem over my life even when I was very little. Even his choice of words was prophetic: he didn't say Loftus would applaud or cheer, but said it would 'roar'. Today whenever I get the ball in my hands the crowd chants my name, and the sound of it reverberating around the stadium is like a roar. How significant is that?

I was told by a friend of my dad that they went up to the west stand of Loftus, and he saw my dad, speaking from the top of that stand over the field, saying something like this:

> Thank you, Lord, that the time will come when my son will play for the Springboks and Bulls in this stadium, and their applause for him will be like a roar.

My Uncle Dawie earlier mentioned the letters my dad used to write to me to encourage me. I've managed to find a few, and here they are.

22 July 2002

My son,

Congratulations on Saturday's match against Pietersburg. The standard you maintained in that game is in line with your talents. You are definitely not fit enough to be eighth man and will have to do some roadwork. It was good to be able to talk to you, especially about the guys' lifestyles that serve as a mask to cover up their feelings of inferiority – such a noisy bravado of 'macho-man' with which they want to make a statement. Be yourself – stay humble, with a small hint of sarcasm, but without harshness. Just say something like, 'One day you will know or understand where the great lions walk.'

You are very busy all the time with your activities. You have to develop a more earnest hunger for your purpose. Paul says in the Bible, 'Lay aside those things that hold you back and run the race to win.' He says further, 'The athlete that runs a race must keep his eye on the goal and not be distracted by things of this world.' The way you played on Saturday was in line with what we have discussed recently. YOU HAVE TO TAKE MORE INITIATIVE. Go for it. Don't be afraid of making mistakes. You need to break up the scrum from behind with the ball, and run a few opponents out of the way. YOU HAVE TO STAY MORE OUTSIDE, as this is where your runs came from on Saturday.

REMEMBER, REMEMBER what I am telling you now. If there are already a few men at the loose ruck, STAY, STAY, STAY, STAY outside until the ball comes out to you. If the whistle blows, you can go and take your place to scrum again. You have to have three good gym sessions this week. Continue with the spiritual focus you experienced at the Craven Week with Joey. Do not be ashamed to testify about God. That is all that counts. Be strong in the Lord. Be humble in your actions – be friendly towards less important people and children and continue to be the gentleman that you are now.

I am very proud of you and I'm convinced that you are bound to make Loftus roar.

Dad

August 2002

My son,

Well done. Your team is in the final. A school final is like any other final, such as a Currie Cup or Olympic final. You may not be playing in a big stadium or in front of the whole country on TV, but the basic rules and principles still remain the same. Prepare yourself as if you are playing in a Currie Cup final and tell yourself that somewhere in the game you will make your statement. Above all else, be still in your soul and seek God. Play for Him and always give Him the glory.

I pray that the Lord will bless you during this week and throughout the weekend.

Dad

March 2004

My son,

It was great speaking to you at the HPC yesterday. I have still not seen any video footage of your last two matches, but according to you it went well. For the past four or five weeks I have been VERY worried about you. I am thankful that I could have a conversation with you regarding the dulling of your senses. The Bible is full of examples of this topic. It is a virus that creeps into the thoughts of man and opens the door to PRIDE. Normally no one notices, except the people that are closest to you.

Recently (since the middle of January), every time I've asked you something about the team, or where you are going to be playing, or who is playing in which position, you've answered me in the tone of, 'Now that's a stupid question!' Lately I've been apprehensive to phone you as it sounds as if I am wasting your time. Or maybe I have seen it in other famous boys – their fathers are an embarrassment to them. If this is the case with me, I will withdraw completely and not be an embarrassment to you. I'll just pray for you in the background, like your grandmother Cielie. You are standing in front of the door of the most significant moments of your life. Just as fast as you got there, even twice as fast, you could fall from there.

My prayer is that you will continue to be the model son that we all know. I pray that you ask God to forgive you if the pride virus has got hold of you, and that the preparation in the next two weeks will be a total FOCUS on excellence, as you have had before in your life. The whole world's eyes will be on you in the next month.

I love you and I'm very proud of you. I know that you will become one of the all-time greats.

Love, Dad

There are many more lessons for life that my dad taught me, but they are too many to list. He had such a wonderful attribute of conveying positivity through his words. He was never afraid or shy to give me a high five, hug and big pat on the back, and even a kiss, whenever he came to my schoolboy games. I really do miss him, but I know that the best way I can honour his memory is to live a life that he would be pleased with. I hope that the new generation of man will not struggle with affection as the older did.

There is tremendous power in a daddy's hug: it is amazing, especially with girls. In my experience, girls often use their dads as a measure when looking for a husband.

My thoughts

- As a father, never be afraid to show affection to your children.
- Always speak words of blessing and favour over your children.
- Pray over and affirm your children with positive words filled with hope for their future.
- Fathers, always lead your children by example.
- Always be proud of your own children – they are yours!

CHAPTER 7

Setback to comeback

Our greatest glory is not in never failing, but in rising up every time we fail.

Ralph Waldo Emerson

With my dad now resting in peace, I had to face the reality that I would take his place as the man in our family. These were pretty big shoes to fill, but his passing away really gave my lifestyle a jolt. I had to get back to the plan that he and I had worked out for my life. In early 2005, my arm had healed successfully and I was back in training with the Bulls. I was able to use my dad's death to motivate me back to where I had fallen from.

I was feeling great training alongside the likes of Victor Matfield and Bakkies Botha, and other great Bulls players, whom I had looked up to when I was younger. Training with these great players at the highest level was a real inspiration for me, especially after such a testing year, with an injury and my dad passing away. Now I had the chance to measure myself against some of the best players in the world in strength, speed, skills and conditioning by playing in the Super 12 competition. I thought that everything was falling back into place and people were again beginning to recognise my talent.

Heyneke Meyer, who was the coach at the Bulls, helped me a lot in my preparation to get myself in a position where I could knock at the door for a place in the Bulls starting line-up. I was back to playing at wing, where I had last played for the SA Under-19 team, and got my chance to play for the Bulls again. However, in a pre-season friendly against the Sharks in February 2005, I injured my ankle. I still managed to go on tour and got a chance to debut, and in the process become the youngest Super 12 player. My chance finally came against the Highlanders in Dunedin, New Zealand.

That day, 11 March 2005, I played wing for the Bulls wearing the number 14 jersey. As the game progressed at Carisbrook Stadium, I could not perform at my best and had a really bad game. The reason for my dismal performance was at the captain's practice the day before, I pulled my quadriceps muscle by kicking a ball without warming up, but didn't tell anyone. I was too embarrassed to say anything about it before the game as I was also nursing a half-healed ankle. There was so much hype about me making Super 12 rugby history by being the youngest Bulls player ever that I didn't want to pull out at that stage. This was going to be my breakthrough year, and nothing was going to stop me. I had been sidelined with injury for almost a year and I was not going to let a small 'niggle' on my thigh stop me from playing.

It was not possible for me to get into full stride, and I was suffering. The only consolation was that we were also not performing very well as a team, and that was reflected in the final score of 23–0 against us. I was very disappointed. It wasn't much of a debut for me, as I ended up being taken off at about the 60- or 70-minute mark. Of course I was partly to blame, as I shouldn't have played – my immaturity quite evident there. As a consequence of my injury I was sent home.

My injury also caused me to miss playing in the SA Under-21 team, which I really wanted to. As I began my road to recovery in 2005, I had to start playing university rugby again at Pretoria, and go back even further to play a whole year of club rugby. I was actually glad of that, because it reduced the pressure on me, and I got a chance to really enjoy the game again and build my confidence. In fact, it allowed me to find my feet again after all my injuries. I played on the wing for the the University of Pretoria (Tuks) for a whole season of Carlton rugby and for the Bulls Under-20, where I scored nine tries in six games as we won our cup that year. Those performances caught the eye of Heyneke Meyer, who allowed me back into the Bulls squad for 2006. But he had other plans. He moved me back to the forwards.

Dad's death was a start and set me in the right direction, but it didn't get me closer to God. I would still go to parties, but after his death was doing it much less and getting drunk less. But a feeling of emptiness would envelope me every time I awoke with a hangover. Every time I got drunk, the emptier I felt and the more I knew this was not who I am supposed to be.

A true friend sticks closer than a brother

At that time in my life my rugby career was being revived, but that was only because my heart was being purged. God started sending people into my path to help me find my way back to Him. One such person was Keegan Fredericks, who also played wing for the Bulls and was a man full of faith, with a wonderful passion and fire to his character. I can remember him coming to minister to my roommate Danie and me, and telling us stories from the Bible. I must apologise to Keegan, because at that time we weren't all that keen to hear his stories; we would wait eagerly for him to finish, as we had made our own plans.

Keegan's positive influence eventually began rubbing off on me, and today he is still a mentor in my life. We attend the same church and are great friends. I am grateful for his faithfulness to the task of spreading the Good News. His persistence in inviting me to church paid off. God started working in my heart with specific people: Keegan was one of them and another was Rudi Boonzaier. We had been good friends all the way back since primary school. Rudi would minister to me like Keegan did: we would argue a lot, but as good friends, and I'll always try to justify some kind of stupid argument. I appreciate my friends and am grateful for the good friendships I have. I like this story about two friends hiking out in the North American woods, because it illustrates, in an amusing way, what a true friend should *not* do:

The two boys in their trek stumble across a really angry grizzly bear that begins to chase them. These boys instinctively choose to run away from the bear, despite the well-known fact that grizzly bears can outrun people. One of the boys realises this and shouts out to the other boy ahead, 'Why are we running when we can't outrun the bear?' The boy ahead responds, 'I don't have to outrun the bear, just you!'

I pray that never happens to anybody, but I'm sure you get the point I'm making. True friends stick with each other through thick and thin. If I had to choose a friend to be with when confronted by a grizzly bear, I would probably choose my good friend from the Boks and Sharks, Tendai 'Beast' Mtawarira. If he started charging it's probably the bear that would be doing the running away!

Seriously, I'm glad that when my life was heading down the path of self-destruction, God was able to send people to me to warn me and guide me. At that time, through all that I had endured, I was ready to receive the truth about my life.

It is said that when the student is ready, the teacher appears! Through Rudi's influence I began getting into the Christian lifestyle. I would attend home meetings with him and even visit different churches. I was like the prodigal son in the Bible, and I knew that I was running away from the truth. I am grateful for the events that happened in my life, which gave me the chance to consider what I was living for and where my life was going. I was tired of running away from the truth all the time, and being too afraid to make a decision, because I thought it was too big a sacrifice to make. But, believe me, you reach a point when you don't care, and that's where I was. I knew that I had to change my life and turn away from the destructive path I was on.

There's a saying I like that highlights the problem of lacking direction:

If you don't know where you are going any road will take you there, and you are on the quick road to nowhere very fast!

What this teaches me is that we have to be deliberate about where we want to end up in life. That's where planning is important. If you don't have a plan, you won't have a good idea of where you're going. This is a real big problem that I believe many people face, and as a result they don't realise the great potential that is within them. This reminds me of the story of *Alice's Adventures in Wonderland*, when Alice comes to a fork in the road and doesn't know which route to choose, so she asks the Cheshire Cat:

'Would you tell me, please, which way I ought to go from here?'
'That depends a good deal on where you want to get to,' said the Cat.
'I don't much care where –' said Alice.
'Then it doesn't matter which way you go,' said the Cat.

In order to know where we are going, it is always important that we write down our goals and what we want to achieve, and have a plan for our life.

Born again: My salvation in Jesus Christ, 11 September 2005

One Saturday night I got drunk again at a friend's party, and the very next morning I realised that I couldn't carry on like this. It was certainly not the life that I had planned or that I wanted any more. That morning I went to church.

Our church was small back then and there were only about 100 people in the school hall where the service was held. After the preaching of the message, the pastor called out to those who felt their lives were not right with God. I raised my hand as I felt things weren't right with me and God. I didn't think they'd expect me to stand up or do anything, but the pastor asked everyone who did raise their hands to come to the stage. I thought: 'No way that I'm doing that!' But luckily one of the ushers came and asked me if I'd like to go to the front. That was it. I knew there's no turning back now and I went forward and surrendered my life to Jesus that very day. I cried as I did that, knowing that deep within, this was the thing I've been running from. I didn't care what my friends or anybody else thought, because I was making a choice for my own life and taking a stand for what I believed was the right thing. And believe me, that little stroll to the front changed everything!

I didn't want to be lukewarm any more, as I realised that was not pleasing to God. My whole life I had been a 'lukewarm' person – someone without the conviction to stick to their beliefs 100%. I believe that if you don't stand for something you will fall for everything. All along I had thought I was a Christian, because I had grown up in a Christian home, but that did not make my standing with God right.

My life was slowly changing for the better as I began walking with God and attending home meetings. The more I read my Bible, the more I began to understand the plans that God had for me. One of my favourite Scriptures says that very thing:

> 'For I know the plans I have for you,' declares the LORD, 'plans to prosper you and not to harm you, plans to give you hope and a future.'[26]

I could make a difference because I was forgiven and made new. For the first time in my life I was able to experience the love of God over me. And what I had, I wanted my friends also to have, so I started to tell them about the love of God that came to earth through His Son Jesus Christ. You can tell that I was quite passionate! Of course this didn't sit well with my mates, so they didn't want to party with me and be my friend any more. I used to invite them to come to church with me, but naturally they didn't respond at first. However, when they started seeing the changes in my life, they became a lot more receptive to coming to church with me or hearing me talk about the Bible.

I believe that making the right choices is only effective if you have a point of reference that guides your decision-making. For me personally, the Bible is that reference point. The things I believe about myself are underpinned by what it says. We all need to have something that keeps us honest, and offers us correction and guidance. I accept that we are all different and as such have differing views and opinions, so the choice of what to use as a reference is yours – but make sure it is solid and reliable.

At that time I also started praying a lot for my sister, Johanni, as her life was not right with God. This resulted in us arguing a lot, but I also kept inviting her to church and to our 'home cell'. She did eventually come to a home meeting, and was pleasantly surprised to hear from my friends there that they had been praying for her. Soon she made a firm decision to follow Jesus as well, and things in her life started to change for the better. After a few months she began playing music in the church and really growing in her new-found faith in God.

My own life was getting back on track, and not long after that, in October 2005, I met my wife, Juanné Weidemann. For this I am grateful to my friend Rudi, who attended her church. He was the matchmaker and told me that he knew a girl who was just the right one for me. I told Rudi that I had stopped going to church just for the girls, to which he replied that this was different, as he felt she could be 'the one' for me. This aroused my curiosity enough for me to go to church and see her for myself. My first response to Rudi on seeing Juanné was, 'Whoa, man!' I found Juanné very attractive, I mean, I couldn't help myself staring at her! But more than that, I could sense that she also had a love for God and she had a real pure heart, which is beautiful. We would see each other at her home group meeting during the week, and we talked more and more. After a few weeks, I invited her to my church and she liked it very much.

There is a lot to share about our relationship, and I'll do so later. But now back to rugby! At the end of the year I went to the Bulls pre-season training camp in George, in the Cape. This was no holiday camp, but rather a gruelling, intensive preparation for the coming season. It was designed to test us to the maximum and make us true champions: we would enter the camp as boys and leave as men, very fit men.

2006: Back in Super Rugby for the Bulls

The next year, 2006, saw the Super 12 become the Super 14, when the Western Force and the Cheetahs joined the competition. It was also the first year for the new Super 14 trophy (which now, incidentally, resides at my beloved Loftus).

I can confidently say that once I'd got my life right with God, my career started to soar. Within a year of my Super Rugby debut, I was back in the Bulls and playing in my favourite positions as a loose forward, at six, seven and eight, and coming off the bench regularly for Coach Heyneke as an impact player. By that time, rugby was no longer a 15-man game, but had evolved into a 22-man game, with the bench a major factor separating the top teams. For that whole season, I only started in about three games, and the rest were off the bench. But it was a great feeling to be a part of the Bulls that season, when we finished fourth on the table to qualify for an away semi-final against the Crusaders. Playing the Crusaders on our home ground is no easy affair, but confronting them on their territory in Christchurch is an even taller order. We packed our bags and headed for that semi-final against the team with the best Super Rugby record, also remembering an earlier loss to them at Loftus earlier that season, when we went down 17–35.

That semi-final unfolded as expected. The Crusaders, spurred on by their home supporters, were formidable opponents. We went down to them for a second time that season, 15–35, the only consolation being that I managed to score a try in that semi-final. The Crusaders went on to defeat the Hurricanes 19–12 in the final at Christchurch, in misty conditions.

When I reflect on that season, I acknowledge that Coach Heyneke Meyer continued to be a big influence on my career and backed me a lot. He would motivate me by asking questions like, 'Do you know how good you are?' He would compare me with another player and ask, 'Who's the best?' Then I would answer, 'I am.' Coach Heyneke was a great motivator and visionary, a man who knew how to find talent and develop character in a player.

2006: Under-21 World Cup in South Africa

My performances that year for the Bulls in Super Rugby caught the attention of the South African Under-21 coach, Peter de Villiers, who recruited me into his team for the Under-21 Rugby World Cup, in which I played as a loose forward. Under Peter as coach I really enjoyed my time with the Under-21s. Even though we didn't win the competition, we had a great time.

A memorable game for me was our semi-final against New Zealand, which we won. They were attacking in our half, about ten metres out, and I was at centre, filling in for our injured centre, who was off the field. New Zealand attacked and from a line-out we turned the ball over, I got hold of the ball and ran through for a 60-metre try. We won that game 40-23 to reach the final, where we met the hosts, France.

We were pretty confident of our chances against France, having beaten them in the group stages in the pouring rain. But they were up for it, especially in front of their home crowd: they made very few mistakes, and they put us under pressure. I scored a try similar to the one I'd scored in the semi-final, this time running about 50 metres to score. Even so, we lost the match. I was disappointed, because I'd lost out previously at the 2004 Under-19s World Cup in South Africa, when I'd broken my arm, and now our Under-21s had lost.

My performances didn't go unnoticed, though, and while playing for the Under-21s I was summoned to the senior Springbok training camp at Bloemfontein for fitness testing. I got there at lunchtime and had a chance to chat with some Springboks: Schalk Burger, Juan Smith, Percy Montgomery and Os du Randt. They were all really friendly and greeted me as they ate lunch. I actually felt a bit overwhelmed. After meeting the guys I went for my testing at the gym.

My bench press (maximum) result was 170 kilograms, and for the 40-metre sprint my best time was clocked at around 4.8 seconds. I also had to do a repeated sprint test. Feeling confident after the test results I went straight back to the Under-21 squad. (I did these tests before we went to our Under-21 World Cup.)

Dream come true: My Springbok selection

My hard work and good performances looked set to reward me. My performance at the Under-21 World Cup drew the attention of the Springbok coach, Jake White. He was also keen to have well-conditioned athletes in the Bok side, and Jake mentioned my physique, strength and speed as key factors that had caught his eye and led to his calling me in for those fitness tests.

The moment that my dad and I had dreamed of and planned for was about to happen. It was only right that I was at Loftus when I received the fantastic news that I was a Springbok. This was where my dad had prophesied from the west stand that his son would be a Springbok. That prophecy came to pass as I was having one of my regular chats with the Bulls doctor, Tommie Smook, when he received the email announcing the Springbok Tri Nations squad for 2006. He was elated, and showed me that 'Pierre Spies' was on the list. As the news sank in, I thought of my dad and how proud he would have been. I was sad that he was not there to celebrate my selection with me. My emotions overwhelmed me and I began to cry.

Tommy and I prayed together, and I thanked the Lord for this fantastic opportunity. My career had reached the highest possible plane, and I was so excited. Once the team had been announced to the media, my phone didn't stop ringing. The first person I called was my mum, and then I spoke to Juanné and my sisters. I had an amazing sense of achievement, filled with promises and excitement.

Later that day I got a call from Peter Jooste, one of the Springbok selectors. He congratulated me, then told me to pack my bags and get ready to join the squad for the Tri Nations tour. Once reality hits, you realise that Test rugby isn't just a matter of rocking up and expecting everything to be fine. I was 21 years old, and I had to learn that lesson very quickly.

My Springbok debut: A match to forget

My debut for the Springboks was going to be in the away leg against the Wallabies in Brisbane, a venue that has not been very successful for South African teams. I must admit that still today I don't know how we could have lost so badly: we were hammered 49–0. On paper we had a good team, with John Smit leading us, but we just didn't fire I guess. Even in my favoured eighth man position, I played poorly. That will probably remain the worst game I have ever played for the Boks.

As the new kid on the block, I was targeted by the senior Wallaby players. They knew it was my debut and wanted to 'welcome' me to the Test arena. They aimed the usual banter at me whenever I got the ball, to put me off my game, things like shouts of, 'Take his head off, take his head off.' Every time I got the ball I kicked it straight into touch when it was supposed to be an up and under. Even the Aussie fans were giving it to me and not making my debut pleasant. I thought to myself, 'This isn't happening', but it wasn't a bad dream, just a real baptism of Test rugby.

All credit to the Wallabies, the better team by far that day. Australia's backline was superb, with man of the match Matt Giteau scoring two tries, while Jeremy Paul, Greg Holmes, Chris Latham and Mark Chisholm also scored. Australia could have gone even further ahead had it not been for the efforts of Fourie du Preez, who held up both Sam Cordingley and Nathan Sharpe in goal.

Even worse than being a terrible debut, my poor performance resulted in me being dropped for the next two tour games against the All Blacks and Wallabies. You can imagine the fallout from the press and the fans after our humiliating loss. We lost 35–17 against the All Blacks in Wellington, but fared a lot better on our return to Australia in Sydney, narrowly going down 20–18.

In the home leg of the Tri Nations we were hit with two injuries in the space of a week, which resulted in Jake White giving me the chance to make amends for my poor debut. That was against the All Blacks at my beloved Loftus, where I played at number seven. I had a much better game this time, but we still lost 26–45. For a few moments towards the end it seemed as if we might make a comeback: in a great final quarter, our centre, Jaque Fourie, scored twice in a few minutes around the 60-minute mark, after André Pretorius replaced Butch James at fly half. But our late surge was too late, and the result was another triumph for All Black coach Graham Henry.

A week later we travelled to Rustenburg for our next game against the mighty All Blacks. We came back from the dead to end the All Blacks' 15-Test run of success with a 21–20 victory in their final Tri Nations Test for that 2006 season. It took a 78th-minute penalty goal by fly half André Pretorius to secure the long-awaited home victory, after All Blacks number eight Rodney So'oialo was penalised for pushing Victor Matfield as he was standing off a maul.

We scored two tries in that game, with Bryan Habana seizing on an intercept and scoring. I had a hand in the next one when I made a good run, which was finished off by Pedrie Wannenburg, who was playing in my favoured eighth man position while I played blind side at number six. In this game I knew it was do or die for me, and I had to put in a worthwhile performance to cement my place in the team, or else I would be out. The danger man among the All Blacks was their captain, Richie McCaw, and I had to make sure that I was all over the park to make life uncomfortable for him. My efforts that day were duly rewarded when I picked up the man of the match award.

That victory was enough to silence our critics, and it gave us some much-needed momentum heading into our last Tri Nations game against the Australians at Ellis Park. At half-time in that game, the scores were tied 3–3. In the second half, when we were awarded a penalty from a driving maul close to the Wallabies line, Fourie du Preez took a quick tap and slammed through a host of stunned Australian defenders to score a magnificent try, which Pretorius converted to give us a 19–10 lead. Breyton Paulse scored another try and we held on for a great 24–16 win, a fantastic finish against the side that had thrashed us in our opening game of the Tri Nations. We had sweet revenge, ending on a high with two straight wins against the All Blacks and Wallabies.

After my last two Springbok outings, people were excited about the way I played, and I went into the Currie Cup season on a high. I actually made my Springbok debut before my Currie Cup debut. In my first two games I was named man of the match, and I put in some really good performances that season, scoring lots of tries. In the final we had to settle for a draw against the Cheetahs, and that was the first draw of my professional career. We all know what a draw feels like.

I was chosen for the end-of-year Springbok northern hemisphere tour, which is always tough. This one was particularly hard because many of our senior players were being rested in anticipation of the upcoming World Cup, and we lost two out of our three games. I was one of the youngest players on that tour, and I found it challenging, being my first tour in Europe. Our first Test was against Ireland at Lansdowne Road, and to celebrate 100 years of Springbok rugby we were wearing exact replicas of the jerseys worn by the 1906 touring side. Incidentally, it was on that tour that the name 'Springboks' was first used. The playing strip consisted of a green jersey with a white collar, blue shorts and blue socks. The 2006 game didn't turn out to be a good centenary celebration, as we lost 15–32. The only highlight for me in that game was tackling both their wings out into touch right before the goal line in cover defence.

In our next match, on 18 November, we faced England at Twickenham in the first of two consecutive Test matches, and went down narrowly 21–23. It was in that match that I suffered a posterior cruciate ligament (PCL) injury to my knee, which luckily didn't need an operation as it ended up being a second-degree tear. This injury did, however, keep me out of the next Test the following week and also the early part of the 2007 Super Rugby season. It happened in the last seven minutes of the game, when I was running across the defence line and felt my knee click.

Unfortunately, at that late stage in the game, there were no substitutes left, so I had to finish the game, and got smashed in a tackle as the English players noticed that I was battling a bit. I was sent home for treatment, together with Butch James and Jacques Cronjé, and for two months I had to use a knee brace and undergo rehabilitation. We won the Test at Twickenham on 25 November 25–14 in our first victory at Twickenham for nine years. It's always good to finish the year off on a high with a win, but sadly for me I also finished the year with an injury.

CHAPTER 8

Preparation for glory: 2007

Nothing can stop the man with the right mental attitude from achieving his goal; nothing on earth can help the man with the wrong mental attitude.

Thomas Jefferson

With the World Cup in France coming up in September, 2007 was going to be a very big year for rugby. There was talk of all three of the Super 14 countries wanting to rest some of their top players. All Blacks coach Graham Henry wanted New Zealand's best players to miss some of the Super 14 games, and received the approval of the five New Zealand Super 14 franchises. These players would go into a special 'conditioning programme' for the first seven weeks of the Super 14 competition. John Connolly, the Wallabies coach, was interested in doing the same, but the South African Rugby Union decided against resting any top players. This made for an interesting Super 14 before it even started. My recovery from the PCL injury progressed well, and I was able to rejoin the Bulls team when they came back from tour. I felt good and played really well as I came back from the injury. We posted some good wins that year, beating the Stormers 49–12 and the Blues 40-19, both at Loftus. Playing the Blues is always special, as they are quite physical and play a good brand of rugby. It was the first Super Rugby season in which I was a proper starter.

Record game against the Reds

In one very special game, we set a new Super Rugby record with a winning margin of 89 points against the Reds. Having lost to the Crusaders in the away semi-final in Christchurch the previous year, we knew how important it was to secure a home semi-final. Before our last preliminary-round game against the Reds, our management did their homework and worked out that we needed to beat the Reds by something like 72 points to secure a home semi-final. Playing against the Reds at Loftus, with all the media hype and the prospect of a home semi-final riding on the result, was going to be one of the greatest games of my career.

During the weeks of preparation, Coach Heyneke Meyer sat us down and looked at the advantages we would have against the Reds:

- They were a young and inexperienced team.
- This was their last game on tour.
- They had already suffered some bad losses during the season.
- They would certainly not be in a good frame of mind.
- They would battle to adjust to playing at altitude on the Highveld.

These were all valid points that certainly gave us the edge over them even before we had played them. Then Coach Heyneke asked the players which of us could be counted on to score the tries we needed to secure this home semi-final. He was very specific on what we needed to accomplish, and asked us how many tries he could count on us individually to score, and also who would make the cross-cover tackles. Then he broke it down even further by classifying how we were going to score the tries: how many tries were to be scored from drives, how many from scrums, and so on. He also emphasised that because time was of the essence, we had to run back smartly every time we scored. In that game, every second was going to count.

Bryan Habana, Derick Kuün and I told Coach Heyneke that he could count on us to score two tries each, and we did just that. We kicked off with a bang, and there was great anticipation among our supporters in the stadium, as they all knew what we were up against and what we needed to achieve. Those supporters really got behind us. As we started scoring, the score line seemed to be keeping up with the clock. We scored three driving tries and ended up winning the game 92–3, which proved to be a record margin. The other try scorers that day were Wikus van Heerden (two), Fourie du Preez, Wynand Olivier, Gary Botha, Pedrie Wannenburg and Jaco van der Westhuyzen.

If we had not won by the required margin, we would have had to get on a plane and make the long trip to Christchurch, just like the previous year, to play the Crusaders on their home ground. But now it was the Crusaders who had to pack their bags and get their flights arranged. They probably hadn't thought we'd do as well against the Reds as we did, and expected to play us at home, so they weren't at all prepared when we pulled it off. That long plane trip between South Africa and New Zealand, whichever way you're going, takes a huge toll on your body. The time difference between the two countries is eleven or ten hours, depending on whether daylight saving is in operation in New Zealand.

I believe we had the upper hand as we went into that semi-final. But we knew that we would have our hands full with the Crusaders, and we weren't going to count our chickens before they hatched. Earlier that year they had beaten us 10–32 at Christchurch, so we knew what to expect.

The Crusaders played valiantly, but we had the momentum to grind out a 27–12 victory in a very charged atmosphere at Loftus. Having fallen behind 0–6 to the visitors, we pulled it back to 9–9, but then Daniel Carter scored the third of his four penalty goals following a breakout of defence that he had begun. That semi-final ended up being a contest between the kickers Derick Hougaard and Daniel Carter. We were grateful that Derick kicked more over than Daniel, and we got the victory.

This victory made it possible for us to advance to our first ever Super Rugby final. In doing so we also inflicted the first ever semi-final defeat on the Crusaders in nine appearances at this phase of the competition. Our win achieved another milestone: the first ever all South African Super Rugby final, with us trekking to Durban the next Saturday to play the Sharks, who had eliminated the Blues.

We knew that final against the Sharks was going to be tough, as they had the home ground advantage and we wouldn't have our Loftus crowd to cheer us on, the Pretoria faithful who, for the semi-final, had decked out Loftus in a sea of blue. The Sharks were playing great rugby and had thrashed the Blues 34–18 in their semi-final in Durban. So we knew we were up against a great team and it was going to be a tough battle in the final.

Super 14 final 2007

Before the big final game, Coach Heyneke sat us down and said these inspiring words:

> Great matches are won in the hearts of men.

He meant that it was not so much structure or even talent that was decisive in winning, but rather personal character. The night before the game we had a team session, and we each symbolically took a piece of our heart and pushed it against our teammate's heart. It sounds weird, but it was done to symbolise that we shared one heart. My partner in this was Coach Heyneke.

Even though we have moved into a highly professional environment, I believe it is moments like these that make the Bulls guys unique, such closeness and camaraderie that make rugby in South Africa so great. At our heart is still 'old school' team spirit, which promotes unity and the passion we have to play alongside one another. We count it a privilege to be part of such a great country and to express our loyalty and patriotism by playing rugby, not as a duty or job, but as a passion.

That final was also exciting because before the game, Jaco van der Westhuyzen wrote on a plain white T-shirt, with a permanent marker pen, 'Jesus is King'. He did it so that when we won he could thank the Lord and glorify him. He didn't tell any of us and he also said that he would stand on the crossbar and salute the crowd if we won. Jaco had just returned from playing in Japan, and he looked a bit crazy with his long hair and beard – sort of like Moses of the Old Testament.

Before we went onto the field, Coach Heneke said, 'Take your umbrella to the game and be ready for the rain.' He was encouraging us to be prepared for the result we came for.

Prayer and the cross

We got together as a team before we went onto the field to thank God for bringing us that far and asked Him for protection over us. When we pray before games, it is not for victory, but for the protection of our bodies and that the work of our hands may be blessed. We ask Him to help us glorify Him through our bodies and our talents. We also thank him for the opportunity to use the talents that we have been given.

I take this a step further: whenever I score a try, you will see me pointing up to the heavens. I do this to acknowledge and give thanks to God for giving me the ability to play and to score. I read once that a reporter thought I was doing this in remembrance of my late dad. He was partly right, but he got the fathers mixed up. I was thanking my Heavenly Father not my earthly one.

To further acknowledge God, I and a few other players wear armbands with crosses during games. We do this as a reminder of our faith on the field and a symbol of God's presence, so that we know we are never alone. Knowing this helps me focus better on the game. I look at it as a tangible way to show and demonstrate my faith, rather than just talk about it. More importantly, it is a constant reminder of why I play in the first place: to glorify God. It's also about expressing our faith in public, not being ashamed and covering it up. Apparently that great former All Black Michael Jones made this idea popular, as he is a strong believer in Jesus.

The power of the cross is what strengthens me to overcome my weaknesses. Whenever I see the symbol of the cross, it reminds me of the price that Jesus Christ paid to redeem me. I am open about my faith: I don't like to cover it up and be silent. How can I be when Jesus died openly and publicly on that cross on Calvary Hill?

Game time

It was a very tight game with immense pressure, and I was glad that I had an opportunity to score. It was from an attacking line-out in the Sharks 22. We set the ball up twice and I ran a great line off Victor Matfield, who put me through, and I scored under the posts. What a great buzz, being in my first Super Rugby final and being the first to score! We were up 7–0. But I was soon to negate that try when we had a right-hand scrum in our own half. Both Fourie and I went to the blind side, which resulted in me trying to play the ball over the Sharks' heads, but JP Pietersen from the Sharks grabbed the ball and ran straight through to score. Since we were in an attacking position, there was no one at the back to defend, and he had a clear run to the try line. My elation at having scored vanished at once, and I didn't feel that good at all.

It was turning out to be a really close game – then, in about the 75th minute, the Sharks had an attacking line-out, which we competed for and missed. This meant big problems for us, as it gave them an opening to charge. The Sharks' Johan Ackermann was 37 at the time and a big old monster right there in their forward pack. We missed that ball and they started driving all the way up to inside our 22, where we finally stopped them. They were getting closer and gaining yards and momentum, and finally Albert van den Berg scored in the 77th minute. The Sharks were up 19–13 – but before that try, they had done something that, in my view, cost them the final, and I couldn't understand why they did it: they substituted their most experienced players, Percy Montgomery and John Smit. These were guys you would have expected to be kept on the field, especially as they represented such a wealth of experience. With Percy Montgomery off, either Butch James or Frans Steyn had to kick the conversion. Frans took the ball from Butch and missed it, from in the corner. On the 78th-minute mark we had the kick-off. Our game plan was to keep the ball when we got it, as that would allow us to score. I remember Gary Botha confirming this tactic of keeping the ball in hand and shouting, 'We must believe!'

The Sharks recycled the ball for a few more phases and maintained possession, but then, at around 79 and a half minutes, Butch James kicked away and gave us back the ball. Had the Sharks retained possession for another 30 seconds, they could have won the final. Gary Botha broke through, and I was on his inside, but instead of passing it and keeping the ball in hand as we agreed, he kicked the ball away. Now why would a hooker do that? Then, amazingly, in the 80th minute, the Sharks kicked it back to us, through Frans Steyn. We mounted our final counter-attack with a few more phases. I had a burst down the right and offloaded to Habana, who was quickly shut down. We set up another phase and there's been a lot said about that one: the Sharks turned the ball over but we took it back. Then we moved the ball over to the left, with Akona Ndungane making a good run, but he was stopped about five metres out. Heini Adams moved the ball right and, with a long pass, found our speedster, Bryan Habana, who came around to the inside. Both Bob Skinstad and AJ Venter missed their tackles on him, leaving Bryan to score in the 83rd minute. Hougaard converted and we won 20–19. I couldn't think of a more epic way to win a final.

Jaco had said before the game that he would stand on the crossbar and salute the crowd if we won. True to his word, he did just that – and he put on his famous T-shirt with the words, 'Jesus is King'. Some people were upset by this gesture, but the majority thanked him for making such a bold statement of his faith. I also think his wife said she'll leave him if he gets up unto the crossbar. Thankfully she still loves him very much to this day!

After-match function

We had a team function after the final victory. We were really ecstatic, as it was the first time the Bulls – or any South African team, for that matter – had won the Super 14. There was a little internal prize-giving, at which our team manager, Oom (Uncle) Wynie Strydom, shouted, 'You are a champion!' every time a player's name was mentioned. Oom Wynie then addressed us all and said, 'I just want to tell all you that you are … champions!' The whole team certainly felt great satisfaction at winning the trophy: it was the culmination of all the hard work we had put in since before the season, and winning it in such a way was just amazing. I know that life is about more than winning trophies, but this was something we had worked hard for. All the planning, hard work, fitness sessions, training – in the end success was the due reward that made it all worthwhile.

I was still 21, and about to turn 22 in June. You can imagine what a fantastic feeling it was to be part of a Super 14 champion team at that age. But after the euphoria subsided, my focus had to move on to the mid-year Test matches against England, before the gruelling Tri Nations began. We were to play two Tests against a weakened England team that had chosen to rest some first-team players in preparation for the World Cup in France. It was really a second or third-string England squad that came out to play us, but Test rugby being what it is, no Test was to be taken lightly.

Our first game was in Bloemfontein, where I came off the bench and we beat them 58–10, which was a good hiding. I started in the second Test at Loftus, and scored two tries. This is when people started getting excited about the prospect of me playing in the World Cup. I was named man of the match in that second Test, which was on a winter's day at Loftus that I will never forget, thanks to the scintillating try that I scored. I had also forgotten my mouth guard, and regretted it because I got my tooth chipped in a ruck. Even though in that game we were not playing 'smooth rugby', we were scoring.

We had a scrum on the right-hand side and played to the left, where the ball came out slowly. We were supposed to play that left way, and I came over onto the right side, but our halfback, Ricky Januarie, passed me the ball to his right. I had a one-on-one with the English scrum half and fended him off, which opened it up nicely. I stepped the second and third England tacklers, also giving the fourth and fifth tacklers the slip, and scored a memorable try that had the Loftus faithful roaring. The words of my dad's poem echoed in my mind as I received the rapturous applause from the crowd. It was one of those tries you wished you could score every time. I thoroughly enjoyed it. Again, anticipation of what I might do in the World Cup was building, and people expected great things from me before I could even get there.

Tri Nations 2007

We started off playing two Tests at home. The first was against Australia at Newlands, which we won by two drop goals from Frans Steyn. In that game I was yellow carded and injured, which ruled me out of the next Test against the All Blacks in Durban, which we lost. After this Jake White decided to rest his main players for the World Cup, so we went down to Wellington in the Cape for a training camp at Bishops Diocesan College school. Watching the Tri Nations games on television on Schalk Burger's family winefarm, we saw our second-string team get beaten in away games by both New Zealand and Australia, which made us realise how good our opposition was. Before the World Cup we did a lot of publicity promotions in the media, which created a great deal of excitement for the upcoming tournament in France.

At that stage I was really pleased with how I had progressed through the two years since that horrific nearly career-ending break in my arm. Now I was finally going to be playing in a Rugby World Cup. As each day brought the event closer, the anticipation built up. Having had a successful Super 14 with the Bulls, culminating in us winning the title, I was expected to do great things in France. I had gained selection into the Springbok World Cup squad, and some respected rugby men were touting me as a favourite for player of the tournament. This was well before the tournament started.

Little did I know the drama that was going to be played out before I even got a chance to step onto the plane to France!

CHAPTER 9

Rugby World Cup 2007: Broken dreams

Some of God's greatest gifts are unanswered prayers.

Garth Brooks

With all the excitement of the 2007 Tri Nations over, people were now getting into the World Cup spirit. But about two weeks after our squad was announced, I started experiencing chest pains. Breathing was painful and really difficult: I could only take small, slow breaths. To make matters worse, I began to cough up blood after training. Initially I thought it might be some sort of cut or wound or a broken rib, but never did I think it would be what it turned out to be.

The morning after this started happening, at our training camp in the Cape, I went to the team doctor, who conducted some tests, put me on the treadmill and took an X-ray and MRI scan. That's when the cause of all my discomfort was detected. I was told I had a lung embolism, blood clots in the lung, which was very serious. I didn't understand the magnitude of this announcement, as I was too shocked. Looking at the scans I couldn't believe what I was seeing. The doctor also shook his head in disbelief: he couldn't believe that he was looking at the lungs of a healthy, fit rugby player.

Bad news

That's when he dropped the bombshell: 'You might never play rugby again.'

Everything that I had done for the largest part of my life had been centred around rugby, so you can imagine the shock I experienced on hearing that. But if you thought that was bad – there's more. The doctor went on to say that I could even die. That was the truly devastating part! From being on cloud nine – selected for the Springbok squad to go to the World Cup – I had been hit with shattering news that was more than enough to knock the wind out of my sails. I couldn't believe it – just when my career was beginning to soar. Being a top scorer in the winning Super 14 team, giving great performances in the Tri Nations and against England at Loftus, getting selected into the Springbok squad for the World Cup – and now this?

At first, a jumble of thoughts raced through my mind:

- What, blood clots? God, you must be joking!
- We're on our way to the World Cup, the highlight of my career. This can't be happening!
- I'm walking in your ways, God, and living a healthy life. I look after my body and train hard and don't use illegal substances. So why me? I haven't done anything wrong.

It was also a big shock for the team. I sat down with the team doctor, our coach, Jake White, and the captain, John Smit, and the doctor explained. I asked Jake White to keep my place in the team for the World Cup. I had worked so hard to get there and I still believed that I had a chance to get back in. John Smit was very sad at the news. He saw me as a promising young player, and this affliction, which was a threat to my life and could be the end of my career, came as a big blow to him. Jake White said, 'Pierre, go and get the treatment that you need and make sure you are safe and get well.'

I had all the tests done, and the results were sometimes conflicting: first I'd be told I could play in the World Cup, but then, after enduring more tests and having the new results analysed, the advice would change. In the end, because of the severity of the situation and the high risk posed to my

Early days: our first holiday together – still quite shy and naïve!

Another shot of our great wedding day.

Training with the Bulls.

Holding the hard won Super 14 trophy.

After our Currie Cup victory in '09.

St Andrews golf course with fellow Springboks
...n de Villiers, Victor Matfield and Francois
...ugaard. Me and Vic won on the 18th – what a
...ling!

...weto fever: our two Super 14 games in Soweto
...e special occasions, breaking barriers of old and
...ing the way for the 2010 Soccer World Cup.

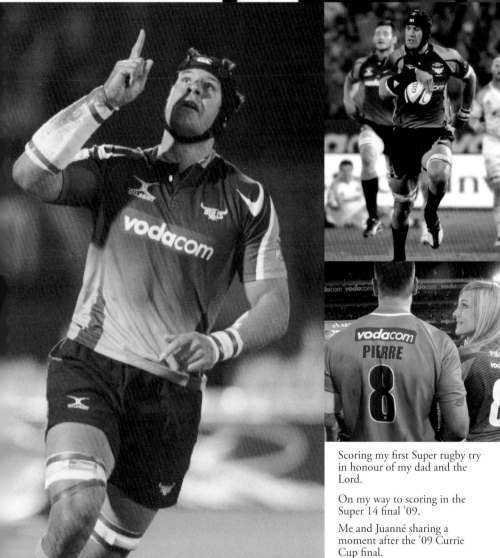

Scoring my first Super rugby try
in honour of my dad and the
Lord.

On my way to scoring in the
Super 14 final '09.

Me and Juanné sharing a
moment after the '09 Currie
Cup final.

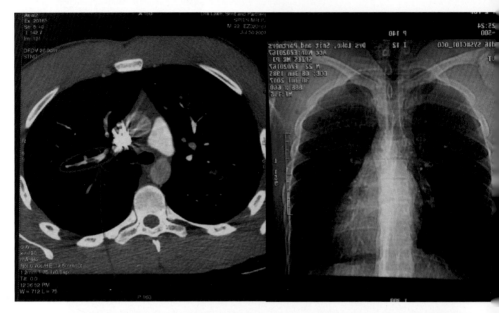

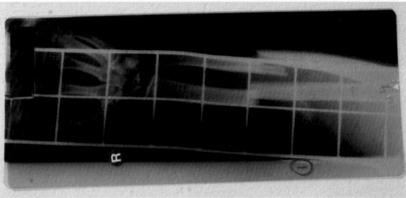

Injuries are part of the game: my lung embolism scans showing my blood clots; my broken arm; and my dislocated finger at the end of '09 which had to be operated on.

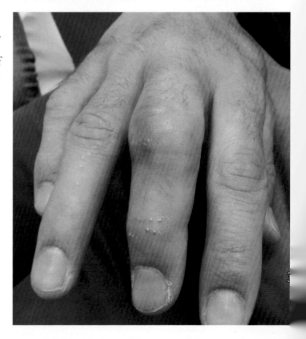

Time for business: me and Fourie singing the national anthem.
On the way to score against the All Blacks U/21.

On the run against the All Blacks.

After winning the British & Irish Lions series 2-1. That trophy is unbelievably heavy!

Doing speed training. Got to train fast to run fast.

A special moment watching the Boks win the '07 World Cup from the stands.

Touring has its perks: sightseeing in London.

Getting baptised in 2006.

Taken on our honeymoon – freedom comes from within.

Myan and me working hard at finishing this book!

Addressing my passion for speed: test driving the Bentley Supersports.

Speaking at a men's breakfast, encouraging them to be strong in tough times.

life, it was decided that it would be in my best interests not to go to the World Cup. The recommendation from the doctors was that I needed to take a course of blood-thinning medication for a minimum of six months. A side effect of these drugs was that if I suffered an open wound, I could bleed to death if I was not treated immediately. Because of this, I was under strict instructions to play absolutely no rugby in that period.

My Bok teammates were really sorry for me, but they could see that I had a peace in me. Jean de Villiers came to me the night before I left the training camp and asked me to record a message to the team. I agreed and Jean left a video camera with me. This is the message I recorded:

> Please understand that you have a great privilege ... [in] being able to play. So enjoy it and give your everything out there. Thank you for your support and encouragement. Take note that I will be back.

I am also grateful for the support that the South African Rugby Union gave me, and the treatment from their great medical team. However, my family felt that we needed to do some of our own medical tests to ascertain where these blood clots had originated. Were they hereditary? If so, we needed to take note of this as a family and all have the necessary tests. So we contacted an independent specialist in Pretoria who subjected me to a range of tests and scans from head to toe to find out where this had all come from. But none of this independent testing could explain conclusively how these blood clots had occurred.

When the news came out that I was not going to the World Cup, I remember getting a call from Joel Stransky. He was sympathetic and supportive, but also wanted to invite me to join his team of TV commentators covering the World Cup. I appreciated Joel's offer and commentated on a few games through the tournament. Around that time the media were having a field day, with all kinds of reports doing the rounds. According to some, I was suffering a hereditary disease similar to the one that killed my dad, and there were, of course, the unfounded, untrue and hurtful allegations that I was using steroids.

Rumours of steroid use

At that low point in my life, I had to contend with these rumours. It was the 'let's kick the man when he's down' syndrome. Even before I developed the blood clots in my lungs, there had been speculation about my physique and build. There were some who felt that you couldn't get a physique like mine without 'extra' help, meaning through the use of banned substances such as steroids. Now, with my blood clots, the rumours received a boost, because it was alleged that the blood clots were a sure sign that I was taking steroids.

Hearing that garbage at this time in my life really saddened me. I always maintained – and I still do – that the genes I inherited from my father, my diet and the effort I put into my all-round training were the factors behind my size and strength. I have one question for these rumour mongers: where are you when I'm putting in all the hard effort in the gym and training my butt off?

But I understand fully that the critics will always be around, and I can't silence them once they have formed an opinion about me. I have learnt that when you try to defend yourself, you can end up looking guilty. The best advice I have received is not to try to defend yourself, and to let the results speak for themselves. As hurtful as the accusations seem, I have learnt this hard truth about life.

I am a firm believer in what Joe Girard once said:

> The elevator to success is out of order. You'll have to use the stairs ... one step at a time.

So I keep my philosophy simple: true champions don't need a short cut to get to the top!

That's the way I live my life, and I can't think of any other way. The benefits you reap from not taking short cuts are plentiful, so I work hard at it. Take it from me, quick results are not always lasting ones and may not always be good for you. I remember reading a story when I was little called 'The Tortoise and the Hare'. The moral of this story was: slow and steady wins the race. To get the body you really want, you need to work hard for it and eat right.

This was a very sad time in my life, but that was where my faith had to override my physical circumstances. I even thought of going back to athletics if I couldn't continue with rugby. At that time of great turmoil in my life, and even though I was questioning God, I felt the peace of God all over me. Immediately I knew that God was in control. I chose to believe God's Word when He says that He has great plans for us and that I have been healed by His wounds.

There is a particular verse that has encouraged me all through my hard times and really puts things into perspective:

> All things work together for good to them that love God, to them who are the called according to [his] purpose.[27]

I had to believe that even though the blood clots had ended my chances of going to the World Cup, they were not bad, because God would work it out for good. My faith taught me that no matter what happens to us, we must always stay positive and focused on God. Whenever I drove to the doctors for tests to be done, I would always put on praise and worship music in my car on the way to the hospital. I would shout out and praise God with a loud voice, regardless of whether my lungs were sick or healthy. I was going to praise God because HE IS GOOD. I had to keep on keeping on in God. I knew that God was going to heal me then or later if it was in His plans.

In faith I remember writing on a big poster 'Healed in Jesus name', and hanging it up in my room. Every day when I woke up and went to sleep, those were the first and the last words that I saw, and I believed them. I knew God had the power to heal me. I can honestly say that my faith was being tested, but I made a decision to praise God whether I stayed sick or got healed. I knew I had to submit to His will. It was an unconditional choice, in the same way as He loves us unconditionally.

I don't play down the fact that I was really shattered at what had happened to me, but the truth is that my faith in God is what carried me through. While all of this was happening, a huge pillar of strength to me was reading the Bible. One particular book that I found comfort and hope in was the Book of Job. For those who are not familiar with his plight, Job was a wealthy man with a wife and children, and a godly man. Then, within just a short while, he lost everything, his wealth and his children, and he also endured horrific boils on his body. I liked Job's response when news of all his losses was made known to him:

> Then Job arose, tore his robe, and shaved his head; and he fell to the ground and worshiped. And he said: 'Naked I came from my mother's womb, and naked shall I return there. The LORD gave, and the LORD has taken away; Blessed be the name of the LORD.' In all this Job did not sin nor charge God with wrong.[28]

What an amazing response! 'I came naked and I am going naked, the Lord gives and He takes away, Blessed be His name.' Those words penetrated right to my heart and made me realise that even though my world seemed to be was falling apart, I should be grateful for what I already had. God had given me good health and the ability to play rugby, and if He wanted to take that away, I was fine with it. I would continue to praise Him. I was reading about Job in my room, which I figured was the safest place for me to be. As I read, I began to realise that even though Job was in favour with God, bad things still happened to Him. Job always defended God and never said a bad thing about Him, even when people saw him suffering and questioned where his God was in his time of pain and suffering. Instead Job continued to praise God:

> Then his wife said to him, 'Do you still hold fast to your integrity? Curse God and die!' But he said to her, 'You speak as one of the foolish women speaks. Shall we indeed accept good from God, and shall we not accept adversity?' In all this Job did not sin with his lips.[29]

That really motivated me and encouraged me not to speak against the will of God. The words of Job and his great wisdom were inspiring, but, more than that, it made so much sense. Why do we only praise God when things are going well, but when adverse situations befall us we complain and are upset with God? It saddens me when people blame God for the bad things that happen to them. One of the questions most commonly asked by people who are sceptical about God is:

Why does a loving God allow so much evil and wrong to take place in the world?

Like so many people, I have struggled with this question, because it pertained specifically to my own life at that time. Only by coming to terms over time with something terrible that you have experienced can you understand the role God plays when tragedies occur. When bad things happen to any of God's children, God is grieved and suffers with us. When people ask, 'Where is God?' in all the tragedies and suffering, the Bible tells us that He is right there with the people who are suffering. A famous Christian writer asked this poignant question:

> When belief in God becomes difficult, the tendency is to turn away from Him – but in heaven's name to what?[30]

There is a lovely poem called *Footprints in the Sand* that highlights very well the point that God has not abandoned you. In the poem, when things are going well, the narrator notices two sets of footprints in the sand and acknowledges that God and she were walking together in her good times. Then, in the bad times, she notices that there is only one set of footprints. So she gets upset with God and asks Him why, in her bad times when she really needed Him, He abandoned her. God's response is that in her bad times, she sees only one set of footprints because He was carrying her. That was what I had to realise – that in the midst of my troubles, God was right there with me. As a Christian I believe that in faith, God will never leave me or forsake me.[31]

The Book of Job was coming alive to me, and the words that I read spoke straight to my heart. It was as if God was sitting right there with me in my room and speaking to me Himself. I loved this other response from Job:

> Though He slay me, yet will I trust Him.[32]

In the end, the Bible says that as a reward for Job's faithfulness, God gave him twice as much as he had taken away from him:

> And the LORD restored Job's losses when he prayed for his friends.
> Indeed the LORD gave Job twice as much as he had before.[33]

Job had it pretty bad, but he endured it all with a good attitude. That taught me to love God unconditionally, not based on my emotions but on His word. We are to love God no matter what happens.

During my time out of rugby, I realised that I needed to go out and encourage others who were in need. Throughout my ordeal of having to come to grips with the possibility that I might never play rugby again – and, more seriously, that I might die – I grew closer to God and my faith was strengthened. I had spoken to people before about God, because I had heard of Him, but this trial made me see Him clearly as well. I realise, in hindsight, that it took my near-death experience to make Him more visible to me. Just as Job observed,

> I have heard of You by the hearing of the ear, But now my eye sees
> You.[34]

Right there, through what seemed like my biggest disappointment, God was speaking to me and drawing me nearer to Him. This is why the Bible says, 'All things work for good' – because what may seem 'bad' can, with God, be turned around for 'good'.

Around that time I got a call from the South African Rugby Union asking me to fly over to the South African World Cup team and hand out the match jerseys to the players before the quarter-final against Fiji. I was elated and agreed. I was flown over secretly, so that it would be a surprise for the team, and had the great privilege and honour of handing the guys their jerseys. They were such legends of the game – men like Os, Monty and Victor. I was also given a chance to address the team before the game and I said, 'Stick to what we know and no one can stop us!'

After South Africa's victory in that match, I went out and had some delicious French pancakes with members of the team and then flew back home. I felt very happy for the team and wished them well. I hoped they would make the finals so that I could come back to watch them. They did make it to the final, so I was able to give Juanné the surprise of a trip to Paris to watch the game. One of my sponsors, Adidas, took care of my hotel accommodation, and we were able to do a lot of sightseeing together. The Eiffel Tower was amazing; we even had a little argument on our way up but quickly made up, realising we are on top of one of the most romantic spots in the world! We enjoyed touring around Paris, which is such a great city to explore. It was Juanné's first time overseas, so it was a great experience for her too. We also visited Disneyland Paris, which I believe is a great place for couples to experience together, and not just for kids. I felt like a kid running around from one thrill to the next!

Rugby World Cup final

The big day arrived, and it was an amazing experience to watch the finals as a spectator in the crowd. People didn't recognise me as I was wearing a beanie and a scarf. It was a great moment to be there and watch my teammates win the World Cup. It actually looked quite easy, but I think it would've been a different game if Danie Rossouw hadn't made that try-saving tackle on Mark Cueto. I was really happy for them all, as I knew the effort they had put in to achieve it. After the match I tried to get into the Springbok change room, but at first I couldn't. I had to phone around and finally managed to get in to join in the celebrations with the team. I took some great photographs, and although I hadn't been able to play, being there with them was satisfying enough. I knew there was a greater plan at work. The after-match function was great, and it went on till late; we ended up taking a taxi back to the hotel. A very generous South African benefactor, Johann Rupert, gave us all Cartier watches engraved with our names.

My firm belief is that strength in life comes from keeping to the simple things and holding on to the promise that your best is yet to come. My other encouraging words are that all things will eventually work out for the best. Hold on to these things and you will remain strong and motivated. I could have stayed at home and not been there at the final, but I chose to enjoy the moment with my friends in France. It doesn't matter what's happening to you: even though things might be going crazy, stay focused. With God, you have to believe that 'all things are possible'. Maybe you

or someone you know is going through a hard time, through sickness or
whatever else. Just remember that God will fulfil His plan for you if you
trust in Him. Jesus has used my life as an instrument to reach my family
and friends and help them receive hope and encouragement through the
tough times, and I know that He can do the same with you.

My time of trial in 2007: Excerpts from my diary

10 July

Diagnosis of my lung embolism. Whole day I was at the hospital and
happy to be alive and I know God has a huge plan – read Job today. Why
would I get this before the World Cup – is it ironic and coincidence? God,
you are in control and I will walk in faith. Juanné said we don't accept
it, Satan knows the impact I could make. And how does God see all of
this? God will heal me – I live for you – I am not of this world – protect
me from evil – I am your child, take away my sickness. Thousands are
going to be touched by what God is going to do.

19 July

Spoke to 1200 men at a church in Vanderbijlpark and gave my testimony
encouraging people to trust God and expect good things – and not
knowing I would be receiving the unpleasant news. Eleven days later I
got the news of the blood clots.

24 August

God said I knew what I could handle, and for me it was about souls and
lost people and injured and hurt and divorced, addicted, and not about
glamour, but about souls and reaching out – not about money. Word I
received today was from Zechariah 11:11. (NLT)
    That was the end of my covenant with them. The suffering flock was
watching me, and they knew that the Lord was speaking through my
actions.

28 August

My testimony is getting stronger and stronger and today we found more
clots in my lung. Going to use medication for at least six months and I
know that it is not going to be a quick fix. I believe that God could get me

back to my normal self before the World Cup if He wanted to. All I know is, my life is in your hands, my Lord. I live for you. These lungs only want to praise you. I am healed in Jesus' name. Make my vision larger and more effective. Keep me humble and faithful, but more on fire. In the hottest fires the toughest metals are formed. Juanné is awesome, and God in her makes her more beautiful. God sent Juanné to me – thank you, Lord.

10 September

Why are some people more tested and tempted than others? I will keep on serving you and stay at your feet. I love you, Lord: help me be the salt and you are the great I am.

16 September

God specifically didn't send me to France because His grace is shining upon me.

29 October

What a weekend so far – Bok parade through the country – country has exploded and the players are heroes – Johann Rupert's farm ...

13 November

A lady from my church had a dream of God making a tattoo with a reed on my forehead. It was written in Isaiah 41:9–10 (NKJV):

> *You* whom I have taken from the ends of the earth,
> And called from its farthest regions, And said to you,
> 'You *are* My servant, I have chosen you and have not cast you away:
> Fear not, for I *am* with you; Be not dismayed, for I *am* your God.
> I will strengthen you, Yes, I will help you,
> I will uphold you with My righteous right hand.'

14 November

The slander of me taking steroids made me disappointed. Then I read in the Bible 1 Peter 2:15 (ESV), which encouraged me:

> For this is the will of God, that by doing good you may put to silence the ignorance of foolish men.

At this stage I got back into training, but not contact work. Even now I have surprised some of the doctors, and they think I should not be playing and should be monitored on a monthly basis.

16 November

Started to plan for engagement. Decided to make right with previous relationships so that slate was clean.

My thoughts

- In life I have learnt to make the best of every situation, to look at all the positives and to also take the negatives into account, but not dwell on them forever. For instance, I could have stayed in South Africa and sulked, but I chose to go and be with the team. I would have missed a great deal of joy if I hadn't gone.
- If you can't change anything, make a decision to move on: walk by faith. It is in the simple things where the strength lies. Stick to what you believe, and don't lose faith – don't ever.
- Always focus on what you have and not on what you don't have. Don't dwell on your weaknesses and things that you cannot change. None of the great people did that. If they had, they wouldn't have been able to achieve what they did.
- Stop and sit down and think of everything you have going for you. Always be positive and thankful for what you have.
- The verse from Jeremiah saying that God has a great plan for me and there is hope and a future blew my mind away: 'For I know the plans I have for you, declares the LORD, plans for welfare and not for evil, to give you a future and a hope.'[35] Whoa, I'd never even heard of this before. When I share this with people, most are taken aback and respond, 'Really? God has a great plan for me?'
- Remember, God is for you. Whatever might be humanly impossible, with God all things are possible.

CHAPTER 10

Road to recovery

Let us not become weary in doing good, for at the proper time we will reap a harvest if we do not give up!

Galatians 6:9 (NIV)

While I was on blood-thinning medication, I was permitted to do physical training, but not allowed any contact training. I was in the gym and still training as hard as I could, but with another condition: I was not allowed to train my legs for the first three months of my treatment from September to November, and could only train the upper body. I made use of the facilities at my old high school, Affies, to get away from the media, as they were constantly bothering me for a comment.

A friend and fellow Bulls and Springbok teammate whom I admire is Morné Steyn. He was kind enough to share these words.

Morné Steyn
Bulls and Bok teammate

I first met Pierre in 2004, when he started playing for the Bulls Under-21s, and we all stayed together in the HPC at Tuks. I saw a guy who was friendly to everyone, especially the newcomers coming in from

other places. He was still young, but already showed signs of being a
great leader in the making. The thing that impressed me most about
Pierre was his work ethic. You will always see him doing extra work
on the training field and in the gym (which is why he looks like Arnold
Schwarzenegger). He is a great role model for the younger guys in his
approach to training. His performance on the field is a direct result of
what he puts into his training.

I will never forget that try he scored against the Crusaders at Loftus
in May 2009, when he received a pass from Fourie du Preez inside
our half and outsprinted everyone in his 60-metre burst: even the
Crusaders backline couldn't catch him. Then, against the Chiefs, he
took an intercept pass near our 22 and did the same thing, outrunning
everyone to score at Loftus again.

Even more impressive than his talent on the field, off the field he is
just as talented and arranges Bible study to keep us encouraged and
focused on why we do what we do.

I observed how, after his dad's passing, his relationship with God
became stronger and there was a change for the better in his life. He
also became the man in his family for his mum and sisters. After the
blood clots in his lungs were discovered, I saw a change in him when he
realised how fragile life can be. I can see that he appreciates that God
has given him another chance, so he makes sure that he lives for God
in everything that he does.

December 2007

For the first time in three months I could start running and working out
my legs, and I was allowed to go down and join the Bulls at our George
training camp on 4 December. This was going to be part of my second
three-month stage of recovery. I was really eager to regain my fitness and
strength and went too hard, I think – I overdid it. This resulted in my
body being really strained: my hip flexors and legs were the stiffest they
had ever been. Despite the pain (which eventually went away), I really
enjoyed that training camp, where, for the first time after being diagnosed
with pulmonary embolism, I was allowed to have a full training session on
my whole body. I was still warned off contact training, so I avoided that
altogether, but being back in the team was awesome!

January 2008

With the training camp over, I was uncertain about when I would ever play again. That time away from the game had made me think hard about life, and I decided that this was the year I would propose to Juanné and finally place a ring on her finger. My mind was made up: she was the woman I wanted to spend the rest of my life with. But at the beginning of January 2008, I was greeted with more unpleasant news when the doctors treating me told me that I would need two more months of medication.

Though I was disappointed that my comeback to playing rugby was going to be delayed, I trusted the advice of the doctors. I knew that they had my best interests at heart, so I did what they advised. I was not going to risk my life by disregarding what the doctors advised. One of the things that I have learnt through life is to be patient, as my time will eventually come. I like what Thomas Edison said about this:

> Many of life's failures come from people who didn't realise how close they were to success when they gave up.

I had already endured so much. I was not prepared to go against the doctors' orders and not take the medication. I trusted God for healing, but also for the wisdom he had given to doctors.

I was still going regularly for medical check-ups to monitor my progress. Remember, the doctors had not given me much hope of returning to rugby. They'd said it was impossible, that I would never be able to play again, as most people with blood clots never get off the medication. But God is moved by faith, not by anything else. After more check-ups and testing, I was given the all-clear to play rugby again. Yes, we humans have limitations, but with God all things are possible. After six months of medication I received my miracle:

GOD HEALED ME!

God showed His great love and mercy to me and answered my prayers. What He did for me I know He can surely do for you or anyone else. It may not happen immediately, but keep holding on and believing in faith.

My time for playing rugby again did come, when I was announced in the starting line up for the Bulls to play the Blues in Eden Park, Auckland, New Zealand, on 29 March. I was overjoyed at the faith the Bulls showed in my ability by giving me that chance to play for them again.

As much as the year 2008 was special for me, as it marked my comeback after I almost died, it was also the year of many changes in the Bulls. Our regular captain, Victor Matfield, was away in France playing club rugby, and with Heyneke Meyer taking up a more senior role, we also had Frans Ludeke taking over as head coach. And let's not forget that 2008 was also marked by many rule changes to the game of rugby. There are some rule changes every year, but 2008 saw quite substantial ones:

- Corner posts – The corner posts were moved. Also, a player would not be in touch if he was touching the corner post, unless he was also touching either the touchline or ground over the touchline.
- Quick throw – A ball could be thrown backwards on a quick throw-in rather than having to be thrown straight.
- Offside line – The offside line would now occur immediately once a tackle was made.
- Scrum half – At the breakdown, the scrum half could not be touched unless he was touching the ball.
- Scrum – During a scrum, the offside line would now be five metres behind the hindmost foot of a scrum (with the exception of forwards in the scrum, and each team's scrum half).
- Breakdown – For not entering the breakdown through the gate, or foul play, the punishment would be a free kick (with the exception of forwards in the scrum, and each team's scrum half).

I came off my medication two weeks before playing in my comeback match. As it was the first game in which I would be taking full contact, I was a bit apprehensive. You can imagine the thoughts running through my mind, as I didn't know how my body would respond. I had done the necessary preparation and put in the hard work at training, so it was not as if I was going into that game unprepared. During my time off from competitive rugby I had learnt the valuable lesson that everyone is replaceable, never mind how talented you are.

Prior to my comeback game on that tour, we had lost 8–40 to the Reds and 27–40 to the Chiefs. I hoped my return to rugby would change that losing streak, but mine was not to be a fairy-tale return. We ended up losing to the Blues in Auckland 21–23, thanks to a drop goal by All Black Nick Evans in the last minute. Even though it is always gut-wrenching to lose, it felt great to be playing again and I was truly thankful to God for the privilege of doing so.

The day after that comeback game, my muscles were really stiff from having played 80 minutes, and I had also picked up a shoulder injury through a tackle by the Blues' match winner, Nick Evans, which was aggravated when I fell awkwardly afterwards. The physio and massage treatment, combined with sitting in hot baths, worked, and I recovered well enough to make our next game, against the Western Force in Perth.

That game in Perth we also lost, again in the last minute. I realised that when you aren't good enough, and when you aren't where you're supposed to be, then you obviously can't expect to win. What made it even more disappointing was that we lost by just one point. I played in two of our last four games on tour that season, and I can honestly say, based on our results, that we seriously missed Victor Matfield, who had taken that season off to play in France for Toulon. All credit to Fourie du Preez for doing his best as team captain, but anyone who has played with Victor would agree that what he brings to the game with his talent and experience at the line-out is really special.

The other factor to consider in 2008 was the change in the head coaching position at the Bulls, with Heyneke Meyer stepping down and Frans Ludeke taking over. Frans, like Fourie du Preez, did his best to fill his predecessor's huge shoes. But I guess these changes were too much for the team to handle that year, especially while we were getting accustomed to the rule changes.

This year, 2008, was a year of building and new beginnings for the Bulls. We were glad when our lack of form changed the following year, but before that there was one more crushing loss to endure.

Our engagement: 8 April 2008

On our return from that tour, we were given Monday to Wednesday off, and that was when I planned to propose to Juanné. This was a very special moment in our lives, and I go into more detail about it later in this book. But the Hurricanes, whom we faced the following weekend, weren't sentimental at all, and put a big damper on my engagement celebrations when they thumped us 50–22 – a game I am sure Bulls players and fans would love to forget. Having come off a terrible tour where we lost our four last games, and having just become engaged, I expected things to pick up, especially playing at home in Loftus. But no, Ma'a Nonu and his teammates had to spoil everything. Nonu himself put in a terrific performance, grabbing two tries that day.

Even though I scored in that game, we were outplayed and beaten on every front by a rampaging Hurricanes outfit that gave us a real shock. The alarm bells began ringing, and the very next week Frans Ludeke got the team together for an urgent planning session. We discussed our dismal performances and areas where we had gone wrong, and were urged to improve our performances and, most definitely, to pick up our game. We had to face the fact that our chances of making the last four of the Super 14 tournament were gone, and we now had to focus on the coming Currie Cup season.

At that team meeting, in the wake of our terrible loss to the Hurricanes, we resolved to win every subsequent game. Getting together seemed to have a positive effect on us: from that point we didn't lose a Super game for the rest of the season, and eventually finished eighth. I guess it was also motivated by the board telling us they would double our match and winning bonuses for every game. As for the next Currie Cup, we trained really hard and put in a great performance, having learnt from our poor showing in the Super season. It was also good to have Victor Matfield back with us, having returned from Toulon. We were rewarded for our hard work by making the Currie Cup final, only to lose to our arch rivals, the Sharks.

My return to the Boks in 2008

I was ecstatic to be selected for the Springbok squad to play the upcoming Tests, and grateful to be part of the international set-up again. Having suffered the blow of being told, 'You will never play rugby again,' it was an awesome feeling to be back at international level. But even though I was back in the Bok team, my selection came in for heavy criticism. It seemed that people's expectations of me in the Super 14 had been very high, and I'd been expected to score 50-metre tries in every game. I'm glad that I had learnt to deal with criticism and was able to put this to one side, because I was overjoyed to be back playing for the Springboks.

Just as the Bulls had had to face coaching changes, so too the Springboks were under a new coach, Peter de Villiers, who took over the reins from Jake White. Like the Bulls' Frans Ludeke, Peter had big shoes to fill. The South African rugby public were sceptical about how the Boks would perform in our first game that year against Wales, in Bloemfontein, especially because a lot of the senior guys had not played under the new coach before, and they all needed to find their feet. This doubt was aggravated when Peter de Villiers chose to start with the giant 2.08-metre lock Andries Bekker instead of the ever-reliable and faithful Victor Matfield, who was on the bench. But Peter saw Victor's impact when he came off the bench, and he started the next game.

In Peter I have seen a man who is big enough to implement what he sees is best for the team and not try to impose himself, which is similar to the quality I see in Frans Ludeke. His aim in starting with Bekker in preference to Victor was probably to give Bekker some Test experience at that stage.

I scored a try against Wales to mark my comeback to the international rugby scene. It was fantastic being back in the Bok squad, and scoring made it even more special, especially when we went on to win the game. In that game Luke Watson, Juan Smith and I were the loose forwards, and we were a formidable trio. I admit that I enjoyed that game, especially as it proved I was right to trust in God for my return to the Springboks. As a precaution I had to do more medical tests after my first comeback, so I missed the Test against Italy in Newlands, which we won convincingly on a very wet day.

Peter consistently backed me up, supported me and believed in me. He selected me again for our next game against Argentina. In that game, we were so far ahead that I played on the wing for a while, and I also scored. I remember the try well: we turned the ball over and our winger, JP Pietersen, hit a gap and chipped the ball ahead. Conrad Jantjes, JP and I chased it. I had a favourable bounce and the ball sat up nicely for me to grab it and go over to score. During that game I experienced some pain in my chest. I was concerned and immediately coughed on my hands to check for traces of blood. I breathed a huge sigh of relief when I saw that there was none – probably just muscular pain, phew!

In the Currie Cup final that year against the Sharks we were really chasing the game and lost 9–14. I was under a bit of pressure as Ryan Kankowski was playing really well, so I had to be on top form to secure my place in the Bok side. Ryan and I are good mates and we enjoy the rivalry for the number eight jersey. He's a talented player and really friendly.

End-of-year tour 2008

Playing Wales in Cardiff is always special, as the Millennium Stadium is such a great venue, and nowhere else in the world are both teams' national anthems sung so beautifully with a full choir and orchestra. It's so good you almost want to sing the Welsh anthem with them! The roof of the stadium can be closed, which helps when it rains. We almost lost that game, as we were leading comfortably but eventually won by just 20–15. Again I was under pressure to perform as my place was at stake.

Our next game was against Scotland at Murrayfield, where we played horribly in the first half and were down at half-time. What is it with us and Murrayfield? John Smit was really annoyed by our performance and told us at half-time that it would be an embarrassment if we lost. We were motivated and charged up for the second half, and came back to win the match, which had proved really tough going in the beginning with Jaque Fourie again finishing for a great and vital try!

I had a great game in terms of ball carries and tackles, and was enjoying my comeback. The end-of-year tour of Europe is always great fun, as there are beautiful places to see, and we can embrace the cold weather in the knowledge that when we return to South Africa there's a nice, hot summer waiting for us. It just takes us a bit longer to get a tan when we return! We can enjoy the excellent European golf courses, and the people are always friendly.

From Scotland, we set off for London to play England. This was billed as a grudge match, because of our last meeting at the World Cup final, so there was a lot of hype before the game. John Smit gave us each a note to encourage us, and let us know what he expected from us. As we were about to go onto the field, he asked for a quiet moment with the team away from management. He spoke to each of us individually, telling us what he expected of us, which was really motivating. Afterwards we prayed as a team, and then went out into the stadium. This turned out to be another of the great games I played in, which we won 42–6. We played England off the park and earned the huge winning margin. It was also a great day for our supporters in England. It's always great to give them a victory so they can go to work on a Monday and rub it in as only fans can do!

Jaque Fourie scored an absolutely amazing try. Danie Roussow, Bryan Habana, Ruan Pienaar and Adi Jacobs got the others. Let's look at each one in turn.

- Danie played in the place of the injured Juan Smith at number seven, and bulldozed his way from about five metres out, taking three England tacklers with him, to score right by the post. This was a display of sheer awesome power from one of the most versatile and talented forward players I know.
- Pienaar charged down Danny Cipriani's kick and scored an easy try under the posts.
- Adi Jacobs ran through the English defence, sidestepped an England defender and held off the English winger to score. This was after Toby Flood handed us a line-out following his pass to 'no one'.
- Jaque Fourie gathered the ball after a clearance from Frans Steyn and outran the defence to score.
- Bryan Habana capped the tries with a clinical finish in the left corner after the ball was worked over from the right.

It was great to finish on a high. I was supposed to stay and play for the Barbarians, but couldn't, as I was going to get married. Yes, Juanné had accepted my proposal. I was so grateful to God, as I'd had a tough year coming back from my injury and returning to the playing field. I was looking forward to taking it to the next level in 2009 – and, of course, tying the knot.

CHAPTER 11

Power of team

No one of us is more important than the rest of us.

Ray Kroc

In a team sport like rugby, the success of the team depends on all of us working together. While you may be a talented individual, there is no place for individualism in a team sport. It's about working together and sticking to the team game plan. That's important, because you can't go onto the field thinking you can just do your own thing. In rugby there are no lone rangers, and whatever success I have achieved has only been through being a part of a team.

I am truly blessed to be a part of the successful Bulls and Blue Bulls teams in Pretoria, particularly because my dad played for them too. We have a unique culture of family that is fostered among players and management. Our reputation as one of the best teams in our competition is thanks, I believe, to our support for one another – a support that is not restricted to the playing field.

One is too small a number to achieve greatness.[36]

I would like to share with you my thoughts on some of the teammates I've had the privilege of working alongside in the Bulls and Springboks. To keep it short, I'll deal with just a few players and coaches. First, the Bulls.

Victor Matfield

He is massive – and I'm not just referring to his two-metre frame. His influence on my rugby career has been huge. I have learnt so much from the way he approaches the game, in his conditioning and life in general. With his passion for the game, he'll make a great coach when his playing career comes to an end. He is very professional; in fact, he wouldn't have lasted this long if he were not. He is one of the fittest guys in the team, which makes it all look so easy, and it's hard to describe the special presence he has on the field. The experience he brings to the team can't really be quantified. Not having him around in 2008 was a major factor in our poor Super 14 campaign. He never panics, or at least doesn't look like he does, and he brings calmness to the team on the field.

Victor has had an amazing effect on my life personally, and I have been deeply influenced by how he lives his life. He is great with people and also very family-oriented – a dedicated husband and father who loves God and his fellow beings. He is the type of guy who is always willing to help and treats everyone the same, no matter what their status. He has been captain since I began playing with the squad, and I have noted his distinctive way of playing with and speaking to the team. He instils great belief into the team.

Fourie du Preez

Fourie is similar to Victor in many ways, with his great rugby mind and mental strength. What he may lack in physical size he more than makes up in mental capacity. His passes and box kicks are among the best I have seen. His decision-making on the field sets him apart as one of the best number nines to have graced the rugby fields of the world, and he is an amazing player.

Like Victor he has aided my rugby career greatly by the way in which he approaches the game. That's where I have learnt a lot from him. People think he is a quiet guy, but privately he's actually very talkative and funny. His nickname is 'Oom Boet' – or that's one of his many nicknames! We have been the eight and nine combo at the Bulls for a while, since 2007, and I always feel secure when he is at the base of the scrum. We have a good understanding of the way each other plays the game, and that is a huge help.

In 2010 Fourie had to undergo shoulder surgery, and the Springboks missed him hugely, particularly his decision-making. He needed to get his shoulder fixed, and it was the right time for him to do it. He plays a huge part in the momentum of the game.

Bryan Habana

It is his amazing ability to make something special happen out of nothing that has made Bryan the player he has become over the years. He is also a great guy off the field, and always willing to give back to the community and make time for them. His world class showed in the way in which he turned the game round in the dying seconds of the Super 14 final in 2007. In a tight game, with nothing happening, he made a break from nowhere and won the game for us. We had a great time playing together, and I wished him well when he headed off to start a new life in the Cape. We certainly do miss him, but his departure has allowed players like Gerhard van den Heever and Francois Hougaard to step up.

Bakkies Botha

I believe that Victor and Bakkies have been the world's best locking combination for a number of years. It will be a long time before another locking pair achieves what they have done.

Bakkies's accuracy in cleanouts and line-out takes, and his sheer aerial dominance, are what set him apart as the world's best in a number four jersey. Very few guys can move a ruck like Bakkies can. Because of his physical 'hard man' style of playing, he gets the short end of the stick quite often, as evidenced in the 2009 British and Irish Lions tour. Bakkies is a special athlete, being very fast and strong for his size, with a rock-hard temperament.

I know Bakkies as a loving family man and someone with a sincere love for God. However the media might portray him, he is well respected for his abilities, even among opposing players. Not all of the rumours about Bakkies Botha are true, but he is definitely one of the jokers in the team. He is the one guy in the team you don't chirp, because he will always go one better in return. He also has a great testimony, so I'm always encouraging him to write a book about where he has come from.

Morné Steyn

Here is a great example of a person who has worked really hard and kept his head, staying focused and waiting patiently for his opportunity. That opportunity came in 2009, when he made such huge strides in becoming such a great fly half. He is also a humble man who has grown in his faith and is always willing to help other people and give glory to the Father for his talent. A down-to-earth lad from Bloemfontein, he's always joking and being one of the funny guys. It was a special moment for the country when his penalty won the British and Irish Lions tour for us from about 60 metres. He came on as a substitute and took that kick as calmly as can be – and the rest is history.

He is also really dedicated and one of the fittest guys in the team. He, Fourie and I have been the eight, nine and ten combo for a while. For me, being surrounded by quality players like Morné makes my job so much easier. When we take the pressure off each other, allowing us to play well as a unit, it helps us all.

Here are some of the crucial kicks Morné has taken for us over the years:

- 2006 Currie Cup final – He converted from the corner to level the score so that we went into extra time. The match ended in a draw.
- 2009 Currie Cup semi-final – He kicked over a 77th-minute penalty at Newlands, on the corner just inside the opposition half, putting us through to the final, which we won.
- 2009 Lions tour at Loftus – Who can forget the match-winning kick that sealed the series for us?

Like the unique family culture of the Bulls, the Springboks share something similar. Even though we have our domestic rivalries in the fiercely competitive Currie Cup and Super Rugby seasons, those are laid aside when we don the green and gold, as we embrace each other in national unity. There are many Bokke that I could talk about, but as with the Bulls, I'll pick just a few.

Juan Smith

Juan, Schalk and I share a pretty close on-field relationship due to the fact that we form the loose trio of six, seven and eight. Juan earns respect by the way he plays, which shows the kind of person he is. He is a no-nonsense type who gets the job done and is solid as a rock, a player you want in your team because just having him around is encouraging. It's a joy to play with him, because when you're under pressure, you know he has your back covered. He is a classic man and he'll probably become the Mayor of Bloemfontein in a few years!

Schalk Burger

What can I say about Schalk? He is a national symbol in South African rugby and an amazingly talented player. He has a wonderful personality and is always friendly. I enjoy playing with him and learn a lot from him. Schalk's work rate is tremendous. The effort I put into my gym workout, Schalk exceeds in his usual wine route! But that seems to work for him. One thing about 'Schalla' is that he doesn't take life too seriously and is always in to have a good time.

John Smit

When I speak of John, I think of his great career and the pillar of strength he has been for South African rugby. He was able to withstand all the criticism and lead the Boks to glory in the World Cup of 2007 and the Lions tour and Tri Nations competition of 2009. He is truly a wonderful guy and an amazing leader. I think he leads the team very well and has a lot of advice to offer to the players. I have personally learnt a great deal from how he manages the media.

John's inspirational talk before our England match at the end of 2008 helped us smash them 42–6. I can't forget his great game against the All Blacks in 2009 in Hamilton, when we won the Tri Nations. He explained to me in writing before the Tri Nations exactly why I was in the starting line-up (as I'd suffered a groin strain just before that).

He is an inspirational pre-game speaker, and usually gets us sitting down, with him in the middle talking to us. He personalises his messages to us and usually calls out our names and lets us know what he expects of us. Barney, you legend!

Through my playing career with the Bulls and the Springboks I have had the honour of being coached by great men. Here are a few:

Heyneke Meyer

When Heyneke took over as head coach for the Bulls in 2004, he introduced a lot of structure to the way that the Bulls played. He took the Bulls to the

Super Rugby semi-finals in 2005 and 2006 and to victory in 2007. He was the coach who gave me my first break in the Super Rugby competition, and he wasn't concerned about how young I was. His motto was: if you're good enough, you're old enough!

His belief and faith in me motivated me to go on and become the player that I am. He was a mentor of my early years, and it meant a lot. He had a strong belief in me, backing me and always inspiring and motivating us with his speeches and coaching. Heyneke can spot talent and character and is a coach who believes in character.

He is a great motivator to his players and can bring out the very best in them. He always encouraged us to set high goals that demanded the best from us. Heyneke's achievements with the Bulls, in the context of our underachievement prior to him taking over, were remarkable, and I believe that he set the platform for the Bulls' fantastic performances since then. His time at the Bulls was a real turning point for the team.

Frans Ludeke

Frans had a really tough first year at the Bulls, having to fill Heyneke Meyer's shoes. I enjoy playing under Frans, who has a special calmness about him. He communicates what he wants from us and then supports us in achieving it. He took 2008 to find his feet, and together we learnt a lot and took those lessons into 2009. Frans is a great planner, and as a team we invest a lot of hard work into this crucial area.

Personally, Frans is one of the humblest people I have met. He is passionate and a great teacher, solid in his faith. Even after all our victories, he never takes credit for a win and always takes the blame when we lose. He is so happy with what he has and is a great family man. I admire him for that, and his life is a good example for the team. With him at the Bulls we have won consecutive titles in the Super 14 and one Currie Cup.

Jake White

Jake was the coach who took notice of me and gave me the opportunity to play for the Springboks in 2006. He'd wanted to choose me earlier as a wing. A lot of people took notice of me because of what Jake said about me, and it was under him that I got my break as a player. Jake has done exceptionally well with the Boks.

Any Bok coach will face a lot of pressure, especially with results like those in 2006. Jake and I had a great relationship, and as a youngster I learnt a lot from him. He also had a good relationship with my late father. Jake had endless faith in me and my abilities, and I am grateful for the way he backed me and gave me another opportunity to prove myself after my terrible debut. He has done a lot for rugby in South Africa.

Peter de Villiers

Peter is a very different man from Jake White. He is unique and feels very strongly about what he believes in. He is great with people, and for the sake of the team gives us the freedom to play as we want to and creates an environment for us to do that. He is a down-to-earth person, and I really have to give him credit for creating the best environment for us on and off the field. ·

On taking over from Jake, he received his fair share of criticism. Despite what the media say about him, I admire his faith in God and the fact that he stays strong in the midst of difficulty. It is enlightening to hear him talk about the opposition he faced as a black coach in the early years. I like working under Peter and must say that I enjoy having him as a coach. He has a really good sense of humour and some witty sayings. Like Jake he has a huge belief in my ability and tries to push me to be best I can be. Off the field he always encourages me, and we have a good relationship.

In 2009, at half-time in the second match against the Lions at Loftus, we were down 16–9, and Peter came into the change room. Without getting hyped up – he never does – he told us calmly that we were letting ourselves down and were going to lose the test if we carried on playing as we were playing. The way he said it got us fired up to prove that we were better than our first-half performance. The rest is history.

CHAPTER 12

Juanné: She completes me

Don't marry the person you think you can live with; marry only the individual you think you can't live without.

James C Dobson

The day when I first met Juanné at her church, they had a Chinese guest speaker, Brother Yun, who was famous for his life's testimony as it appeared in his biography, called *The Heavenly Man*. I was with my friend Rudi Boonzaier, and we were sitting right behind Juanné and her boyfriend, listening to the speaker share the amazing story of his life. Yes that's right, 'Juanné and her boyfriend'! I wanted to give Rudi a 'klap' for talking me into coming when she already had a boyfriend. But Rudi calmed me down and told me to play along, as he knew Juanné's boyfriend was not the guy for her.

After the meeting I introduced myself to her and left. I wasn't aware that Juanné remembered me from when I was in Affies and she was attending a rival school, Waterkloof High. At the time she said that she was going out with a guy who had played against me when we played their school at rugby. Juanné said that in my schooldays she hadn't really liked me because she thought I was a 'rugby jock'. She admits now that she had the wrong impression of me then, but says she gained that impression because she used to see me in Hatfield Square, Pretoria, surrounded by girls.

She recalls looking at me and saying to herself, 'This poor guy, I feel really sorry for him.' That's what she says, but I think it was more like, 'Wow, what a hunk, I wish he was my boyfriend.' I'm convinced that it would have been just a matter of time before my 'magic' kicked in and she became my girlfriend.

I see that Juanné is getting angry with me as I write this, so I had better get back to reality. After that first meeting, Rudi invited me to his church home cell meeting, and from there we started to build our friendship. After some time we exchanged numbers and began staying in touch by texting, or texting, each other. We went on our first date, which was actually more like an interview. In order to get better acquainted, we asked each other questions about our families and our likes and dislikes, and we also discussed life in general.

This 'interview' took place the night before Juanné wrote her Science exam, in which she did really well. (Of course I take the credit, as I must have inspired her to do so well.) Our friendship began to blossom and we starting seeing each other often at the end of 2005. At that stage that's all that we were, just good friends, from October to November. I was waiting for her to finish her final year at high school, and knew that it was an important year for her.

When I made a firm commitment to follow Jesus, I gave up my flirtatious ways. I made a promise to myself that my next relationship would be serious, and with a girl that I intended eventually to marry. I knew that my career was going to take off, and I was looking for a wife who would complete me. I wanted a wife who would stand with me even when things got rough – for better or for worse, in sickness and in health, until death did us part.

I was glad that Juanné was similar to me in that we didn't have a love for worldly things. This greatly attracted me to her, as it had been quite rare in my previous girlfriends. Juanné was down to earth, and besides her outer beauty she had an inner beauty, a purity and love for God that 'sealed the deal' for me. I knew that she was the one for me.

This may sound over the top, but as we were both so committed to our faith we used to fast – not from food, but from all physical contact, not even holding hands for a week at a time. The results were amazing, and something that you cannot fully comprehend until you get married. It was tough, and we did have our moments, but we held off from all sexual contact until we were married. Why was it so amazing? Because it gave us a chance to know each other rather than focus on the physical side and lust after each other. If you're serious about dating someone, then it's not just about physical contact: you need to get to know them and how they think. That's what makes a person, not just their physical attributes.

It was after our second date that Juanné and her parents went down to their usual holiday retreat in Mossel Bay, not far from George. This was where the Bulls held their usual pre-season training camp, which was great for us as we got to see a lot of each other, and officially became boyfriend and girlfriend on Christmas Day, 2005. That ended my year off with a really big high, especially when compared with the gloomy start of the year for me, with my injury.

Baptism

Our youth pastor at the time asked who wanted to be baptised, and I decided that it was the right time for me, as I hadn't been baptised before. Often people don't want to be baptised because they don't feel right, but for me it's more about obedience to God. After all, Jesus was baptised, and we are called to follow his example. I learnt to think of baptism as a public declaration that gives you the confidence to stand up for God. There is a lot of liberty and freedom in it. Juanné decided on her own to get baptised – I didn't make her.

So in February 2006 Juanné and I were baptised together with my sister Johanni. We held the ceremony in a pool at the University of Pretoria's Maroela hostel, where I used to do some of my drinking in my days at the HPC. Juanné and I used to go around as a couple when I was invited to give my testimony, and we would speak together at meetings.

When I look back, I realise that 2006 started off very fast, as I was back in the thick of things at the Bulls and away touring for the first six months, not to mention the SA Under-21 World Cup squad and the training camps. Then, of course, things got even more hectic when I was chosen for the Springboks. There was the Tri Nations tour, in which I made my not-so-good debut, and our end-of-year tour of Europe. So it was pretty hectic, and Juanné and I had precious little time together. But we learnt to make good use of what time we did have.

Super 14 final 2007

I didn't mention, when I was describing our Super 14 final victory in 2007, that at this same time, Juanné broke her jaw as she was about to leave for the airport to fly to Durban. She had stopped to visit her brother who was in hospital, in intensive care, after a motorcycle accident. He was in a stable condition, but not looking very good, with broken ribs and a collapsed lung. Seeing him in that state made Juanné feel dizzy, so she went outside for some fresh air. That was when she blacked out and fell forward, breaking her jaw.

She doesn't remember anything until she hit the floor. She was so focused on going to my rugby final that she told the doctor just to stitch her up. She wasn't aware at first that her jaw was broken, but when the doctor said she would have to wait for an X-ray, she knew that she wasn't going to get to the rugby final. Juanné called me at the ABSA Stadium before the match to tell me that she wasn't going to make it. She recovered soon, and we celebrated the victory when I got back to Pretoria. She was really sad that she couldn't make it.

It was great having Juanné with me when I went through the embolism ordeal. She was a real tower of strength to me, and I thanked God for her. When you face the real prospect of death, you quickly realise which are the things that really matter most, and Juanné was clearly one of the priorities in my life. I wanted to get married early, but the timing was not right as she was studying Human Movement Science at Tuks. I wanted us to marry young, as then we could enjoy life together for years before the children came.

The right time came when we returned from our Super 14 tour and were given a few days off from training. It was 8 April 2008 when I popped the question.

The proposal

I needed some help to pull the proposal off, so I recruited my mum and my two sisters. I took Juanné off to a resort country club in Magaliesburg, and, while I kept her busy with a game of tennis, my family got the room ready. Juanné got really annoyed with my sister Steffani, who was my PA at the time, constantly disturbing me on my cellphone while I was on the tennis court.

After that game we went for dinner, and I can remember that there were noisy building works going on at the restaurant. How romantic – the day I want to propose to my future wife, they decide to drill into the wall next to us! As we were walking to the room, my sister called me to say they were not ready and needed some more time. We quickly made a detour and enjoyed a game of lawns bowls under floodlights. Juanné must have thought I was crazy. I was glad when finally I got the message that the room was ready.

As we entered the room, Juanné was overwhelmed with the roses and candles, and asked what was happening. I didn't have the ring in my pocket, so I had to scurry around the room to get it – as quickly as possible, so that I didn't 'lose the moment'. Juanné saw the box I had made up with photos of us on it, and couldn't understand how that had got into the room.

I finally managed to get the ring, and, telling her that my knee was sore, I knelt down at her feet, looked up and said the words, 'Juanné, will you marry me?' Juanné began to cry and laugh at the same time, and, happily, she accepted my proposal. On the ring I presented to her I had engraved, 'Blessed love forever.' But the proposal was not over. I had two bags of salt, and we each took one, opened it and poured both into one vase. We then mixed them together so that there was no way to tell which salt came from which bag. This was to symbolise the Scripture of the two of us becoming one:

Therefore a man shall leave his father and mother and be joined to his
wife, and they shall become one flesh.[37]

The symbolism was: just as you could never again separate the two bags
of salt in the vase, so too would our lives be inseparable. We also took
communion together that night to commemorate the life, death and
resurrection of our Lord Jesus Christ, on whom we were going to base our
marriage. In the box I placed all the love letters we had written to each
other, a spear ('spies' in Afrikaans), salt and slippers (so that Juanné could
kick her shoes under my bed). Right in the centre of the box I wrote this
quote:

Finishing strong!

This was to remind us of how we were to approach our marriage to ensure
that we went all the way and saw out the distance. I had experienced the
divorce of my parents, and I definitely didn't want that to happen to our
marriage. I wanted it to last. And before we got married, we told each other
everything about our pasts, because we didn't want to carry any secrets into
our married lives.

The wedding date was set for 2 December 2008, and the challenge was
to find a big enough venue for all our guests. We were grateful that we had
our pastors and mentors around us to give us great advice. We also began
marriage counselling, to make sure that we gave our marriage every chance
of working.

We managed to get a venue in Pretoria East and engaged a wedding
planner. I had been away for about four weeks with the Boks on our end-
of-year tour of Europe, and got back a week before the wedding. We catered
for 220 guests, so it was by no means a small crowd. Juanné's wedding
dress had a classic style that was simple and elegant. Her bridesmaids were
my sisters, Steffani and Johanni, her sister, Ina Michelle, and three of her
best friends, Carla, Liezl and Elene. My best men were my friends Ben,
Rudi, Danie and Joey.

I firmly believe that marriage is the primary component of the family
unit. Sadly, this principle, which was once the norm for healthy living, is
being eroded away. The values of marriage as the foundation of the family,

not just in our nation, but worldwide, are under attack. To substantiate what I am saying, you need just consider the high rates of divorce and the increase in single mothers, and you can see the state of crisis that marriage is in.

Could it be the bad publicity that marriage gets from society that is the cause of this crisis? The battering that marriage has sustained from recent cultural changes has influenced an increasing number of couples to view this fundamental institution as optional, ready to be discarded and open to redefinition. In this context of marital decline, there is an ongoing feud raging between those who view marriage as a transient human invention – ready for updating and revision – and those who regard it as a natural institution that is fundamental to humanity and essential to a flourishing civilisation.

When I grew up, we were taught that the institution of marriage was good for individuals and society, but sadly, even though I knew this, I still had to endure the pain of my parents' divorce. Knowing something is not the same as practising it. Going through this pain has motivated me to encourage married couples to strive to protect and cherish their marriages. I have no resentment or bitterness towards my parents for choosing to get divorced – and it's really important for children whose parents divorce to remember this. The health of our society is closely linked to the health and well-being of marriages. Not only is marriage essential to society, but the benefits of marriage for individual adults and children are well known and documented. I am grateful for the research that the pro-family not-for-profit international organisation Focus on the Family has done in this area, and happy to present some of their findings here.

Marriage is good for women, men and children[38]

Marriage elevates well-being measures for men and women. Research shows that married men and women enjoy the following benefits:

- Higher levels of physical and mental health
- Longer lives

- Happier, healthier and less violent relationships
- Greater emotional support
- Lower levels of depression and suicide
- Reduced risk of either perpetrating or suffering a crime
- Increased individual earnings and savings.

Marriage elevates every important well-being measure for children. When raised by both biological parents in a low-conflict marriage, more than 30 years of studies show that children are:

- More successful and better-behaved at school
- More likely to attend and graduate college
- Less likely to live in poverty
- Less likely to drink or do drugs
- Less likely to be sexually active
- Less likely to commit crimes or act violently
- Less likely to be sexually or physically abused
- More likely to have successful marriages of their own
- Expected to live longer than children from divorced homes.

There is even a study from the USA estimating that divorce and unwed childbearing alone cost taxpayers more than $112 million a year.[39] This awareness of the important role marriage plays in society is not new. Edward Gibbon, in his famous work *The History of the Decline and Fall of the Roman Empire*, argues that the decline of the Roman Empire was paralleled by a decline in the morality of its citizens. Once marriage is attacked, the family unit begins to disintegrate, and once that happens, then society is left to pick up the pieces.

Even though Juanné and I can still be regarded as newlyweds, I thank God that our marriage is growing stronger each day. Just as I take my rugby seriously and put in the effort to excel at it, so too is it with my marriage. Juanné and I have people whom we trust, who have been married for much longer than us, whom we look up to as role models and from whom we seek advice, more or less like a rugby coach. We are definitely not experts and are always open to godly advice. If you need help and require resources to help you with your marriage or other family-related issues, then I urge you to get in touch with Focus on the Family.

Respect for women

I grew up in a home with three women and I have always respected women. I had many girlfriends, but I never slept around, and my aim was to get married as a virgin. Both Juanné and I were virgins and kept ourselves for each other on our wedding night. Guys, when you are with a girl treat her with enough respect that when you part she will be fine and speak well of you. For everything we do there are consequences. If you indulge in sex before marriage and sleep around, you may not realise what you've done until you are married. You can't go into your marriage with baggage. Guys should see women for who they are and also not succumb to peer pressure.

But enough from me. Let's hear from my wife, Juanné.

To my husband, Pierre

Our first date – or 'interview', as Pierre so aptly put it – was unlike any other. Being with Pierre, I realised that I had found the man I had been looking for my whole life. Aside from his evident physical attributes, there was something more that drew me to him. It was his love for God and the 'Jesus within him' that attracted me so much. At that time I didn't have a personal relationship with God, and being around Pierre made me realise that that was the fulfilment I was also looking for in my life. In the three years we dated, we both underwent an awesome growth process, and I really grew in my relationship with God. We grew together in our faith, as a couple and as individuals.

Before we married, Pierre and I got to know each other well, and not just as a couple but as best friends. From the beginning we decided not to build our relationship on physical contact and to keep ourselves sexually pure before marriage. It was not always easy, but I praise God for helping us keep ourselves pure before marriage, as He intended it to be. We didn't realise the value of this until we got married. There is so much power in saving yourself for your husband or wife. Trust me – it's worth it, a thousand times over. It's never too late to start.

I believe that God sent Pierre into my life to reveal Himself to me and to become the best I can be, and to help me find my true identity in Christ. I learnt so much about God by being around Pierre, especially when he went through his ordeal of having to withdraw from the World Cup squad in 2007. Pierre had worked very hard and was looking forward so much to playing in France, but when the blood clots were found, this was taken away so unexpectedly. The way he handled the shock and disappointment was truly inspiring and faith-building for me. I can remember watching the final game from the stands with him, and my heart went out to him because I knew how much it would have meant to him to be playing out on the field.

When the full-time whistle went and everyone was going crazy, and the team was celebrating and fireworks going off, I immediately thought that he needed to be there celebrating with the team. It was a bittersweet moment for me when the Springboks won that final, because I was happy at their victory, but at the same time I knew how disappointed Pierre was at not being able to play. However, I could see that he had a perfect peace about him as he watched the game. In fact, he did not show one bit of disappointment, and was really overjoyed when the Springboks won. I guess he knew that his best was yet to come. I was just happy to be there with him.

Our marriage has been everything that I could have asked for, and, as Pierre has described it, it is 'perfect'. So far I have learnt that love is not based on your emotions, feelings and circumstances but on the unconditional commitment of the heart! As you grow closer to God and get to know Him personally, you and your husband or wife will grow closer to each other. And that threefold cord is not quickly broken. ('Though one may be overpowered, two can defend themselves. A cord of three strands is not quickly broken.' Ecclesiastes 4:12, NIV)

Pierre, you are my hero, best friend and a husband that exceeds my highest expectations. Thank you for always putting God first in your life and our marriage. Without God we wouldn't be here today. Thank you for understanding me and always being willing to talk and work things through – never compromising on our walk with God, and keeping things simple, which keeps our marriage strong. Thank you for loving me unconditionally and for the fact that we can pray and play together. As we made our vows on our wedding day, be assured that I will stand by you and support you.

With God on our side we can make big plans. Even though we may still be regarded as newlyweds, I pray that we will run this race with perseverance, with God's purpose in front of us (to bring people back to Him) and FINISH STRONG!

I will love you all the days of my life!

Your wife,
Juanné

Thank you, Juanné, for sharing this. I am really blessed to have her as my wife, as she is so multi-talented. She holds University of South Africa (Grade 8) and Royal Schools of Music qualifications in the piano. She also did ballet up to the elementary stage, and is now a qualified Pilates instructor, and runs her own business in anti-ageing and nutrition.

My thoughts

- When you get married, things don't just fall into place. You need to plan for them to be in place beforehand.
- Finances are an area that causes a lot of stress for couples as they don't plan properly, so take the time to discuss this important matter before you marry. Money doesn't grow on trees or fall from the sky.
- Everyone is different and not the same as Juanné and me – so it's important that you pray together and play together. What I mean is that you need to do fun stuff together as that's what brought you together initially, so don't let it die – enjoy the time with each other.
- Juanné is my best friend and that makes things a lot easier as we can talk things through. Communication is important and also the way you communicate. There is no point in screaming and shouting.
- Don't allow little things to destroy your marriage, because it is the 'little foxes that spoil the vine'.

CHAPTER 13

2009: A year to remember

The person who really wants to achieve something finds a way, whilst the other finds an excuse.

Unknown

I was glad to end 2008 on a really good note by getting married to Juanné. I dubbed it 'the year of the gun', because it was the year when I was subject to the most criticism, as it was the time of my comeback from illness. Another reason was that my 'guns' (arms) were the biggest they had ever been, because at the beginning of the year I hadn't been allowed to exercise my legs, and therefore trained my arms extra-hard. It also hadn't been a good year for the Bulls, and we hadn't performed as well as the previous year when we'd finished as champions. Due to my illness I hadn't done proper pre-season training, so while my physique was fine, I did lack a little in fitness. I made sure that to compensate for all the time I'd spent on my arms, I made up for it by spending more time on my fitness in 2009.

In 2009 I trained really hard for the Bulls, and as a team we learnt a lot from our mistakes. Victor Matfield was back, which was a huge boost, and we also planned more and strategised astutely. Now that I was married I was also on cloud nine, as I knew waiting for me when I got home would be my wife, Juanné. So the motivation to excel was even greater. That year I ran a lot in the games, and it paid off, as I was the leading try scorer for the forwards in 2009. We won all our home games, the most memorable being against the Blues, which we won 59–26. That game I scored two tries and set up another two. For my first try I capitalised on a poor attempted chip by Paul Williams and then broke away and sprinted 50 metres to score and stretch our lead to 26–0 after just 24 minutes. The Blues came back at us, but we held on for a convincing win.

We started our tour by beating the Hurricanes 19–14, and in that game Ma'a Nonu gave me a 'welcome to Wellington' high tackle, which the referee spotted and penalised by awarding us a penalty. I checked and found that my neck was still attached, so I carried on. We later lost 12–36 to the Highlanders in gale-force blustery windy conditions in Palmerston North and the Crusaders in Christchurch 13–16. We made up for it by beating the Waratahs 20–6, but went down to the Brumbies in the last minute by one point, 31–32. We scored four tries in that game, so we did earn a bonus point. We sorely missed Victor, when he went back to South Africa for the birth of his daughter, and Bakkies, who was suspended. With 12 minutes to go I thought I had scored the winner to put us ahead 31–22, but the Brumbies had a strong finish to clinch it.

At home we had wins against the Chiefs, Western Force, Cheetahs, and Sharks – the last by just one point, in Durban, 27–26. That game will also go down as one of the best I've been involved in and that win earned us a home semi-final against the Crusaders.

Super 14 semi-final 2009

The semi-final was a match to remember, as we recovered from being 7–20 down to win 36–23. We were chasing the game the whole time, and then we started keeping the ball more, and Morné kicked us penalties and drop goals. With two minutes left before half-time, at 20–20, we kicked on the Crusaders and they countered and chipped. Fourie du Preez caught it and played the ball to me. I stepped Stephen Brett, put my ears back and ran 50 metres all the way to score under the posts, one of the favourite tries in my life. That sent us into the break with our tails up, 27-20 in the lead. Morné had a great game, with four drop goals. It was great to run out eventual winners and head into the final against the Chiefs.

Super 14 final 2009

The Chiefs beat the Hurricanes in the other semi-final and had to travel away to us. We planned well that week, and Loftus was a sell-out. Our fans camped outside the stadium, from straight after the semi-final on Saturday until Monday morning, to buy tickets.

In that finals week it's all about managing your body and making sure everyone is on the same page. The key is to make sure you don't do anything silly and get injured – so no intense training should be done. We went in with a lot of confidence and we knew the Chiefs had travelled a long way to get to us.

The atmosphere at Loftus was electric, and there was a great vibe around the stadium – fireworks before the game, smoke in the air – all leading to the kick-off of one of the greatest finals. The Chiefs scored first with Lelia Masaga, and we had to regroup. We declared that there was no way we were going back, and we knew what we needed to do. It was an unbelievable night of rugby. We played brilliantly and held onto the ball to turn it into points. In the second half we knew we had the momentum going forward, and in the last ten minutes I had my chance when I got an interception outside our 22 from the Chiefs halfback. I opened up the taps and sprinted all the way to the corner for a try. I tried to dive like a wing but it seems I'm not really good at that! It was a great final that we won very convincingly 61–17. A record victory for a Super Rugby final.

There were delirious celebrations. I was elated at scoring a try in that final, and at our winning it. It was the perfect game. I take my hat off to the Chiefs for their grace in defeat. Captain Mils Muliaina, speaking after the match, was very humble and complimented us on the game and the season, and even thanked the crowd and the people of South Africa.

This was our first home final victory, so the after-match function went on till very late, or should I say very early – the next morning. All the families joined us in the change room and we spoke about the game and the season and just savoured the moment. I wanted to stay as long as possible but went home at about 2am. Some of the guys stayed to watch the sun come up from the halfway line, and Victor had the braai going. But I missed out on the sunrise that morning as I was totally exhausted. But Victor gave me a picture of the sun rising, taken from inside the stadium. It was majestic!

British and Irish Lions tour 2009

After all the euphoria of the Super 14 final victory, we had to prepare for the much-anticipated British and Irish Lions Tour. This really special tour happens only once every 12 years, so I was privileged to participate in it, as most players don't get that chance in their international careers.

We went into the Bok camp in Durban and had about two weeks to train and prepare. At that time I also had to write an exam for the Construction Management degree I was studying towards. I missed out on the shark diving that the Springbok squad experienced, but did enjoy the great team-building exercise in a KwaZulu-Natal game reserve. Singer Robbie Wessels came along and played his guitar and sang songs around the camp fire. It was good to relax and unwind, as we knew we were facing a really intense Test series against the Lions.

The team selection had not been finalised, and at that late stage we did not have an open side flanker (fetcher), as Schalk Burger was a doubtful starter because of injury. We could have gone with Juan Smith, Danie Rossouw and me, but the management brought in Heinrich Brussow from the Cheetahs who already played the Lions and fared well against them.

I have never seen anything like that Lions tour frenzy. The media attention, fan interest and performance pressure were intense, because we were the world champs. The Lions were a well-oiled and well-trained outfit, so we had to stick to our guns and play our game.

First test: Durban

We scrummed really well with 'Beast' Mtawarira, Bismarck du Plessis and John Smit. People sometime forget how great a player John Smit is: he can play at loose head, hooker and tight head with the same skill and expertise. For the Lions tour he played tight head, giving Bismarck the hooker role. John was superb against the Lions and led us brilliantly to that series win. Our first try came from an attacking right-side scrum in their 22, from which our backs took it up through Ruan Pienaar, with John Smit diving over and breaking free from Tom Croft and David Wallace. It was game on: we were really psyched up and scrumming well, which meant the Lions were under pressure and conceding penalties.

Jean de Villiers and Morné Steyn made some try-saving tackles, resulting in the TMO (television match official) decision going our way. To use a line from the movie *Any Given Sunday*, it was all about 'gaining inches'. In rugby you need every player's inch to give you the momentum to put the team on a good path to stay focused and finish the game, until the final whistle blows.

The substitutions turned the game around, and luckily we held on to the win. In that instance it doesn't matter how or by how far you win – it was the win that mattered. We needed just one more win to take the series, and we gained a lot of confidence from that game. Our drive was working really well, and when we had penalties we kicked for touch and drove, which resulted in Brussow scoring from a drive from about their 22. It was awesome for him to get a try on his debut. All in all, our forward pack drove, scrummed and executed the line-outs brilliantly, and the Lions were no mean opposition – they were good.

I remember one of the Lions players 'chirping' away at us when they had a right-hand scrum only five metres away from our goal line. The pressure was intense, because in Durban it's quite difficult to kick out, especially from a defensive right-hand scrum close to your goal line. Any player can tell you that this is one of the most high-pressure situations to be in. Our scrum went down and the ball was coming back to me when the opposing scrum half applied the pressure. He screamed at Bakkies and me, calling us 'steroid monkeys' while ripping my scrumcap off my head.

I was taken aback, and actually laughed as no one had ever chirped me like that before, with that degree of insensitivity. I asked myself if this was still part of the game? Was winning so important that he had to resort to that? I thought the game had moved on from personal attacks and insults. I was not fazed by it, but disappointed. I cracked up with laughter when Bakkies responded to the Lions player, 'You know, you have the most beautiful blue eyes.' At the end of the game I made a deliberate effort to shake this guy's hand, but he chose not to let me. Perhaps he was so disgusted at their loss. But I guess those moments will always be part of sport.

Second test: Pretoria

The ice was broken after the first test and the Lions were better prepared. We started the second test at Loftus badly and were not executing our kicks and set plays well. It was in this Test, in the opening minutes, that Schalk Burger was given a yellow card for the infamous 'eye gouge'. Down to 14 men, we were really under pressure. Rob Kearney, the Irish full back, was fielding our kicks well, and we had a tough first half, chasing the game. Coach De Villiers's half-time message was hard and straight to the point: we were letting ourselves down and not sticking to the game plan. 'Let's get out there and finish off what we planned,' he said. We started the second half playing a lot better and had another attacking scrum. Brian O'Driscoll tackled Danie Rossouw and hit him on the blind side: there was a massive clash of heads, resulting in Danie being taken off. Brian O'Driscoll stayed on – I think he didn't know that he was concussed at the time.

Adam Jones, their number three, also went off, which meant that the scrums went uncontested. It could have been part of the Lions strategy, but it ended up working in our favour. O'Driscoll made a wrong defensive choice (probably from still being concussed), resulting in Bryan Habana scoring and bringing us back into the game. We attacked and built some phases, which resulted in Jaque Fourie bumping off Ronan O'Gara and scoring in the corner. It was a try that I consider to be one of the best and most significant I have seen – and it put us ahead. Then Morné Steyn, who had come off the bench to replace Pienaar, converted it from the side. Morné knew every inch of Loftus, as it was his home ground, and certainly knew how to kick there.

When the scores were level at 25–25, Ronan O'Gara kicked up a bomb and chased it, but was judged to have taken out Fourie du Preez in the air. No advantage was played, which was a shame, as the ball fell to Habana, who would have had a good run to the try line. We were given a penalty in our own half. There was deliberation between Victor and John as to which Steyn should kick it, Morné or Francois? John asked Morné, 'Can you do it for your country?' and Morné nodded that he could.

I was praying under my breath before he kicked it, 'Please, God, let him kick it well.' When the ball went over, the whole team erupted and ran over to Morné, who said, 'As soon as I hit it, I knew it was over!' The final whistle blew shortly after that, and we had won 28–25 – and won the series. It was time for celebration. My teammates named me man of the match, which means a lot. They presented me with a stuffed Springbok head, which still hangs in my home. The feeling after that win was amazing and we clinched the series 2–0 right there and then. What a way to win it!

Third test: Johannesburg

We had already clinched the series, so the coach decided to rest some of our first-choice players. I came on as a substitute and played on the left wing, in place of Jongi Nokwe. The Lions led from the start, with Shane Williams scoring two tries. England lock Simon Shaw was sin-binned for striking out against Fourie du Preez and received a two-week ban. It was quite silly, if you ask me, as it was a grubber kick that Fourie fielded, with Simon Shaw chasing after it and falling with his knee into Fourie's back.

The Lions went on to win the third Test 28–9.

I was thankful to have been part of this tour because it was such a rare event – and, more importantly, because we won it. Experiencing this rugby tradition was one of the highlights of my career, and definitely my personal highlight of the international calendar in 2009. But the year wasn't over: there was still the Tri Nations to come.

Tri Nations 2009

Our first Tri Nations game of the season was against the All Blacks in Bloemfontein. We went from strength to strength, winning the game easily. We beat them again quite easily in the second Test in Durban, with Morné scoring all 31 of our points. Next, we faced the Wallabies in Newlands, and won that easily. Then began our tour, which saw us win in Perth against the Wallabies. Our run of good fortune came to a halt in Brisbane, which has proved to be venue that does not favour us.

Over to New Zealand, where we met the All Blacks in Hamilton for our final game, needing just a point to win the Tri Nations. I was a doubtful starter for this game due to a groin injury, and was rested from training. I only did the captain's practice. We started very well and got into a good lead, but the All Blacks came back at us. However, we held off their late challenge to win that game and lift the Tri Nations trophy, making 2009 a super year for me. I had been on the winning team in the Super 14, the Lions tour and now the Tri Nations. We had beaten the All Blacks three times in one year, which was a great feat. That night after the test in Hamilton the guys really let loose and enjoyed the victory thoroughly.

Returning home, we went into the Currie Cup, and that year we made the semi-finals in the Cape against Western Province. We went into the half-time break leading 12–3, but when we returned, the momentum started changing. Province scored a try and were leading when we were awarded a penalty inside their half, close to the touchline. Morné stepped up and did what he does best, kicking it over between the posts. We won the game and looked forward to a home final against the Cheetahs.

Before that final, I had dislocated my right middle finger in a game against the Griquas by getting it stuck in an opposing player's jersey. The finger was strapped up for the final, but it kept getting dislocated, so the team doctor, Org Strauss, had to keep putting it back, and I was also given an injection to numb it. It got dislocated pretty badly, but I continued to play. I went for an operation on the Monday after the final and had a metal pin inserted. That resulted in me missing out on the end-of-year Springbok tour of Europe. I had really wanted to go on that tour, but rested and enjoyed my time with the family, as I knew that the George camp for the Bulls was coming up soon.

After the George camp in December, I was doing some speed work on my own that Christmas Day – yes that's right, Christmas Day! – and I pulled my hamstring. I was really silly to do that, as it meant I missed out on our pre-season training for 2010. It was not a good way to go into the new year.

Juan Smith (Springbok number 7)

The first time I heard about Pierre was in 2005. That year the only man that Jake White could talk about was the monster of a wing that was playing 'eigth man'. I must be honest – I thought to myself, there is no way that a wing can start playing with the forwards. All wings are scared to play with the forwards, but Pierre came on the scene and proved everyone wrong!

The game that I will remember the most was when Pierre played in Bloemfontein against England. Pierre was first receiver off the scrum half and ran a reverse line, handed off the cross defender and side stepped the full back, scoring the best try I have ever seen a loose forward score.

More than what he has achieved on the field of rugby, I see Pierre as being a strong believer in Jesus Christ, and never too shy to talk about his love for God. The guys in the Springbok team call Pierre - 'Pastor' – because he is in charge of all the Bible studies that we have. If there is one word to describe Pierre, I would say 'Mirror', because when you see Pierre you see God's Love, and the way one should live!

The other thing that stands out about Pierre for me is the way he handles setbacks. In a rugby player's career the ultimate reward is to go to the World Cup, and when Pierre was ruled out in 2007, I thought to myself that this setback was going to break him, but Pierre came back that next year stronger, faster and more determined than ever before!

CHAPTER 14

2010: Unity and hope

Sport has the power to change the world. It has the power to inspire. It has the power to unite people in a way that little else does.

Nelson Mandela

This was a special year for all South Africans, as it was the year we hosted the Soccer World Cup. But before that, I believe the Bulls made history and, through rugby, helped forge more national pride and unity. This happened in the Super 14 semi-finals and finals. First, though, here is my review of games I particularly remember in the Super 14 2010 season.

Bulls 50–35 Brumbies

I got a big fright in our second game against the Brumbies at Loftus. I was tackled by their prop, who held me from behind, resulting in my right foot getting stuck and me being bent over backwards. I felt something click and froze in terror. At first I thought I had torn the cruciate ligament in my knee, which usually puts one out of action for at least nine months. I screamed, because it was really painful, but it was also a wailed 'Oh, no!' at the thought of being out of the game through injury again. At that moment JJ, a pastor and good friend, sat right in front of where it happened and immediately prayed for healing from where he sat.

The team doctor came onto the field to examine my knee, and he said everything was fine, it wasn't torn. When I looked at the video afterwards, it truly seemed a miracle that I hadn't suffered anything more serious. Our conditioning coach, Basil, agreed that I was lucky. I was hurt, but nothing too serious: it was a calf tendon injury, which I was quite happy to take rather than a cruciate ligament tear. I was rested for our next game against the Waratahs. Only a few months later JJ told me how he prayed for me and I believe that protected my knee.

Bulls 50–35 Highlanders

This match at Loftus saw Gerhard van den Heever score a brilliant try from our own 22: he danced his way past attackers and ran all the way to score from the right wing. Francois Hougaard and I scored two tries each as we took the Highlanders down. My first try was thanks to a good burst in the centre from Stephan Dippenaar, off which I received the ball and scored under the posts. My second I picked up from the back of the scrum and dotted down with a tackler hanging onto me. We didn't have everything our way in that game – the Highlanders fought back, with Israel Dagg scoring a hat-trick of tries – but we did enough for a win.

Bulls 19–18 Hurricanes

This was a great comeback from us at Loftus. We were 0–12 down after 29 minutes, and showed our strength by fighting back to earn the win.

Playing away, we beat the Western Force 28–15 in Perth and then went over to New Zealand to face the Blues.

Bulls 17–32 Blues

The Blues are a different team altogether, and were always going to be tough opponents on their home ground. I managed to score a 'behind the head no look' try. We were attacking in their half and were on their line. I was on the right wing, yelling loudly to Fourie to pass it to me. He sent a long flat pass, and then I got tackled, but I managed to put my arms above my head and scored a 'no looker'.

How the book began

It was here in Auckland that I met my writer, Myan Subrayan. Myan is a South African Indian pastor living in Auckland, having emigrated there in 2000. He introduced himself as the co-author of *Inga: My Story* by the former All Black great, Inga 'The Winger' Tuigamala. Earlier that year, Myan had sent me a signed copy of Inga's book after reading my testimony in the local New Zealand Christian newspaper. Inga's book is a great read, with some really inspiring material. Myan told me that when he had heard in 2007 that I had an 'incurable' disease, he and his family had prayed for me.

I met with Myan on the Thursday before Good Friday, and he offered to take me to church the next day. Good Friday being so special in the Christian calendar, I wanted to be in God's house that day, so I accepted the invitation and told him there would be two or three of us. I didn't anticipate that when he arrived the next morning there would be 15 of us waiting, keen to attend church. I was pleased that we attended that morning church service in West Auckland, and that I got a chance to share a brief message on the reason for Good Friday.

Even when we are on tour, we know it is important to go to church and have at least one fellowship per week. I enjoy going to the different churches in different countries, and often I'm invited to share an encouraging message. After that church meeting, Myan and I met at the hotel. We got on well right from the start, because of the similarities in our lives, and the passion we both had for serving Jesus. He had written a few other books, and I asked him for copies that I could present to the rest of the team. The guys and I enjoyed the reads.

For a long time I had been thinking of writing a book, but the opportunity didn't present itself until I met Myan. He shared a few ideas for a possible book, and I liked them. I also appreciated that we had a 'similar heart', and for me that was crucial in anyone wanting to write about me.

He happened to be in South Africa in January 2011, because his mum had passed away, so we arranged to meet in Pretoria. Myan, being who he is in Christ, got on well with my family, and began working on the manuscript immediately. The rest, as they say, is history!

Bulls 40–35 Crusaders

Francois Hougaard's match-winning try after the final hooter had gone helped us clinch a late 40–35 victory over the Crusaders. This breathtaking encounter at Loftus Versfeld enabled us to seal a home semi-final. Hougaard was accused of knocking on, but the TV replays proved otherwise. It was a magnificent win, which we all had worked hard for.

We rested some of our players for our next game, against the Stormers, which the Stormers won, with the result that both semi-finals were played in South Africa. Ours, which took place in the newly built Orlando Stadium in Soweto, was to prove a historic event and a milestone on the road to unity among South Africa's people.

Super 14 semi-final: Orlando Stadium, Soweto

In April 2010, while we were in Auckland, one of South Africa's most notorious supporters of apartheid, Eugène Terre'Blanche, was murdered. This threatened to unsettle the country and stir up racial tensions. The Bulls squad in New Zealand got together and tried to think of a way to send South Africa a message that would reassure people and encourage them to continue pursuing peace and reconciliation, but we couldn't figure out exactly what it should be. Now, by virtue of circumstances beyond our control, we found ourselves playing our semi-final in Soweto, because we couldn't use our own home ground. Loftus had to be handed over to FIFA in line with rules requiring all World Cup venues to be handed over to

FIFA's local organisers no later than 15 days before the opening match of the competition.

This practical, administrative arrangement provided us with the message of unity we needed to send to the people of South Africa. In the past, rugby had carried the ugly stigma of being the sport of the oppressor, because in the apartheid era it was mostly played and enjoyed by whites, while soccer was more popular among blacks. But now, for the first time ever, a huge rugby event was going to take place in Soweto. Nobody knew what to expect, and perhaps the background made some people apprehensive, but we had a good feeling about it. At the captain's practice we saw how beautiful the stadium was, and we began to witness amazing scenes. Bulls supporters came to Soweto in their thousands, and they were welcomed by the people of Soweto, who shared food and drink and welcomed them into their homes. An awesome spirit of unity soon dispelled any thoughts of negative reactions. Seeing all of this gave us a real boost before we went onto the pitch for the start of the game.

The atmosphere surrounding our semi-final was a wonderful precursor to the FIFA Soccer World Cup. In the stadium, with the vuvuzelas blaring, it was a really explosive atmosphere, so much so that we found it hard to hear the calls on the field.

Bulls 39–24 Crusaders

The Crusaders started well, retaining possession from the kick-off, and brought on a series of attacks before a turnover allowed us to launch a good counter, which resulted in me scoring a try in the second minute. I received the ball off a ruck from a beauty of a pass by Fourie, to break off a tackler and score under the posts.

Danie Rossouw, playing at lock, went over minutes later, thanks to some poor defence close to the line, but unfortunately the TMO ruled that he had lost the ball in the act of scoring. We put the Crusaders under pressure with our high kicks, forcing them to make some uncharacteristic errors, when Sean Maitland failed to defuse a bomb and George Whitelock caught it in an offside position. Morné bagged the resulting three-point penalty, to put us 10–0 up. Zane Kirchner scored the next try when he followed up a high kick coming off Sam Whitelock's head. It looked comical, but it was a try.

After the half-time break, the Crusaders scored from a midfield scrum, when Kieran Read passed blind side to halfback Andy Ellis, and quick hands from Colin Slade released Maitland, who did the rest to score. Daniel Carter kicked the conversion and the Crusaders faced only a six-point deficit.

It was all over for the Crusaders when Fourie du Preez scored from a bursting run down the blind side from a wheeling scrum. Morné's conversion pushed the score to 33–17 with 18 minutes to go, and that really sank the Crusaders, who had too much to make up. Two more penalties from Morné sealed the game. The young Crusaders lock Sam Whitelock had the final say with a try at the end, but it was too late for the New Zealanders, as we went on to confirm our place in the final.

Super 14 Final 2010: Bulls 25–17 Stormers

Having already played at the Orlando Stadium, we had an edge over the Stormers: we knew what to expect and the condition of the pitch. The Stormers were a little taken aback by the atmosphere. We handled the pressure well and kept the scoreboard rolling, going away to win 25–17.

This was the perfect end to a perfect season. Statistically it was the best season ever for the Bulls, and again the culmination of hard work on and off the field. The Super 14 is a hard competition, and winning it twice in a row is not an easy task, but we did it. I am humbly thankful to be a part of such a great team of people as the Bulls.

In this final we came up against a good friend to many of us, Bryan Habana, who had recently left our franchise and moved to the Stormers. Bryan scored an intercept try in this match – and you could say that Bulls scored all the tries in the 2010 Super 14 final, if you consider him a Bull. When we met up at the Bok camp later that year, he spoke about the great atmosphere in Soweto and how overwhelmed and caught off guard the Stormers had been – especially with the vuvuzelas and the enthusiasm of the Bulls' supporters. It was certainly a hostile environment for the Stormers.

Bryan is a dear friend, and I asked him to share some of his thoughts in this book.

Bryan Habana
Friend and teammate

I first heard about Pierre shortly after I left school. Having played Craven Week and gone on to represent the Lions at junior level, I heard a lot of talk in the change rooms and on the training fields about up and coming youngsters. Pierre was one of those who many players talked about, with comments like, 'He's a phenomenal young player from Affies – big, strong and quick!' and 'This youngster from Affies has got what it takes to be the next Bob Skinstad!' and 'Pierre Spies is going to be South African rugby's next big thing!' From what I heard and gathered from the guys around me, there was huge pressure placed on Pierre to excel even before he made his senior debut.

My first personal encounter with Pierre was in Durban in 2004. He was part of the South African Under-19 team, and, as an up and coming Springbok at the time, I had an opportunity to chat to them. My first thought upon meeting Pierre was that he was a confident young man – maybe even bordering on too confident. I didn't know then what I know now, and I made that assumption based on my first impression. He had the world at his feet and everything going for him, yet he was pretty mature in the way he dealt with all the attention and pressure that the world was putting on him. He just carried on enjoying his youth.

Pierre, the leader

Pierre is one of those people who don't come along often, and are very few and far between. He is the type of person with whom I feel comfortable communicating and sharing stuff outside of rugby. He is always willing to lend an ear and be positive about everything. He is willing to open up his heart to new people and friends, and makes it easy to talk about difficult issues. He is someone whom many players feel comfortable talking to, and is really humble on and off the field. The example of his life is a great influence on me, and he leads by example on and off the field – whether in the gym, the auditorium or wherever else. I can confidently say that it's really great playing alongside him.

Pierre's physicality

He has been blessed with an amazing talent and is able to do things only a few guys can do. He is big, powerful and quick. This he has achieved by working and training very hard, and he has a more demanding work ethic than anyone else I have ever worked with. Pierre is a sublime physical specimen who works extremely hard off the field to make sure that he is physically dominant on the field. The example he sets, both in the gym and on the training field, is one that many a rugby player dreams of following. For a player of his size, he is extremely quick and powerful, and he often leaves backs in his wake. He dominates many of the collisions he is involved in.

Pierre's physical attributes no doubt set him apart from a lot of other rugby players, but apart from his physical presence, he also has a sound rugby brain and makes the right decisions on the field, more often than not. He is one of those players you can always rely on when the going gets tough. The example he sets by his work ethic is truly amazing and something that motivates many players to continually improve.

Pierre's character

As you have already read, Pierre didn't have a great Test debut against the Wallabies in Brisbane in the 2006 Tri Nations. After a fantastic Super 14, Pierre was called up to the Springbok team for a debut Test that was a baptism of fire, and turned out to be our worst and probably most embarrassing defeat ever. Pierre all but went from 'hero to zero'. I must admit that the performance by the rest of the team was abysmal!

Most players don't come back after a performance and result like that. But Pierre never allowed the disappointment of that game to get to him, and he quietly and confidently set his sights on working even harder to retain the number 8 jersey for the Springboks. He put in man-of-the-match performances in the next Tri Nations games that he played that year to confirm his selection to the Boks.

That's Pierre – a man of great resilience. This resilience was clearly evident when he spoke to us before our quarter-final against Fiji in the 2007 World Cup, shortly after health issues forced him to withdraw from the squad. To see his calmness and positive approach to life was tremendously uplifting and boosted our team morale significantly. In the midst of his great trial, he came over and made a difference to us.

One of the standout matches involving Pierre, as far as I am concerned, was the Super 14 final against the Sharks down in Durban in 2007. Pierre had had a great season to date and was earmarked as a vital cog in the Springbok squad for our World Cup campaign. He scored the Bulls' first try, smashing through the Sharks defence with such ease. His work rate throughout that game, and his leadership – even though he was so young – were outstanding and lifted the players around him.

Another highlight was the Super 14 final against the Chiefs at Loftus in May 2009. Here Pierre was one of a number of exceptional players in a Bulls performance that saw them become the first South African franchise to lift the Super 14 trophy. What an awesome try that was, when he outran the Chiefs and scored with a spectacular dive!

Pierre my friend

Pierre has had a significant impact in my life, both on and off the field. He is also someone who, off the field, is open, honest and transparent. Pierre sets an example in the way he leads his life and the principles by which he stands.

In a world where one is constantly attacked for being a Christian, Pierre refuses to deviate from what he believes in. Through his stand for Christ, he gives strength to a lot of players, and others, in their walk with Christ.

I wish him every success for the future!

Looking at 2011, I believe the Super 15 is the toughest competition in the world: 21 weeks of top-class rugby. Any team can be beaten by any team, and the travelling sets it apart from any other similar competition. It is a really pressurised environment, but one that every professional rugby player thrives on, as it allows his skills to be tested against the world's best.

CHAPTER 15

Finishing strong

To finish the moment, to find the journey's end in every step of the road, to live the greatest number of good hours, is wisdom.

Ralph Waldo Emerson

My dad inculcated in me the desire to always finish strong. What good is it if you start a race, or anything else, for that matter, and don't see it through to the end? All the effort you put in at the beginning would be lost. From a rugby perspective, I think of our victory against the Crusaders in the dying minutes of that 2010 Super 14 game, when Hougaard scored, and also the 2007 Super 14 final against the Sharks, when Habana scored right at the end. Both those games we won in the dying minutes. Those are great examples of what I mean by 'finishing strong'.

In life there are times when we stuff up and make mistakes, and that's OK. But what do you do afterwards? The only failure in life is to stop trying. Having read about my life, you will see that I have come short many times, but I chose to never give up. As long as you are alive, you have the chance to make amends. But don't be fooled into believing that you have plenty of time to set things right, because you don't. Sometimes we place so much faith in tomorrow that we forget to live for today.

I could not have foreseen that I would develop blood clots in my lungs before the 2007 World Cup. I had been chosen for the squad to leave for France to represent my country, when out of the blue I was struck down. Who could have imagined that? As Morné Steyn pointed out, my outlook on life changed for the better after that episode with the blood clots. God allowed me to see life for what it really was: every day is a gift from Him, and we are not guaranteed a tomorrow. 'The Clock of Life' is an anonymous poem highlighting the fact that we don't know what tomorrow brings:

> The clock of life is wound but once
> and no man has the power
> to know just when the clock will stop
> at late or early hour.
> This is the only time we own.
> Live, love, work with a will.
> Place no faith in tomorrow for
> the clock may then be still.

No matter where you are in life, it is nearly always the result of choices you made in the past. It is these choices, good and bad, that result in you arriving where you are today. Maybe you don't like where you've ended up, but don't worry! The good news is that, if you want to, you can change your current situation. This process happens one day at a time, but you can start from where you are right now. Most of the good things in life don't arrive by chance, luck or coincidence. In life you'll come across obstacles and problems – you wouldn't be normal if you didn't! But the secret to achieving your dreams and ambitions is to overcome these difficulties by choosing to never give up.

Even when I was going through the blood clots, I learnt an important truth about life. I found that experiencing difficulties was not an excuse to abandon my dreams. I constantly had to make the choice not to give up. I learnt that I could not blame anyone or make excuses for my life; after all, it was my life. No matter how difficult our circumstances may be, we have the power to choose how we respond.

When the doctors told me I was not going to play rugby again, I chose to persevere. I have experienced the highs of winning many trophies and, through my illness, have also tasted the bitterness of almost losing it all.

On the road to recovery I learnt a lot. I am very fond of a principle called 'sowing and reaping': in life, you reap what you have sown. If you sow negative or positive thoughts, you will reap the same. I have written this book to share with you what I have learnt, and it all comes down to this: life is about making wise choices.

As humans, we have limited knowledge of our potential. We think we're pushing the limits, but the reality is that we're not even close to fully utilising what we have deposited in us. I refuse to die wondering what I am capable of accomplishing. My father had a wonderful way of illustrating to us what it meant to make use of our potential:

> He asked us, 'Where are the wealthiest places in the world?'
>
> We replied that they must be the goldfields of Johannesburg or the diamond mines of Kimberley, or maybe the oil fields of the Middle East. He would reply that they were not, and then explain that the richest places in the world were the local cemeteries.
>
> Of course we were baffled as to how graveyards could be the richest places in the world. Then he explained that beneath the soil of the graveyards were the unrealised dreams, songs, poems, books and achievements of the people who had died. These had never been realised because those people had not tried to achieve them, and consequently died with them, taking all their unrealised potential to the grave.

This lesson from my dad blew my young mind away. I learnt at a very early age that one of the greatest tragedies in life is to die with your talent, ability and potential unused. Look at it this way: you deny and deprive the world when you don't use the potential within you, but you are able to bless others when you release it. Think of what a dark world we would be living in if Thomas Edison had not invented the light bulb – if he had died with that invention still within him, unrealised.

I'm told that Edison didn't get it right the first time, or the second, but failed at least a thousand times. However, he didn't see this as failure, and would respond:

> I have not failed a thousand times. I have successfully discovered a thousand ways how NOT to make a light bulb.

What am I saying? Even if you try, and then fail, that doesn't mean you haven't learnt anything, or that you should give up. This is where the heartbreak of life lies – when we settle for average. By doing this we lose the amazing opportunity of revealing what could be within us. Why be average when God has created you to be better? I was brought up not to be average, and I was taught that by being average I would rob God of the potential He had placed in me. Have you ever really sat down and thought about what average is?

Average is the best of the worst and the worst of the best!

Don't die without attempting to release the gifts, talents, abilities and dreams that are in you. Certainly don't settle for being average, but excel and give your best. Don't let setbacks stop you from trying and from having another go. The people who really make a difference and change the world are those who have removed the statement, 'It is impossible,' from their mind and vocabularies. My comeback to rugby after being diagnosed with blood clots could have been called 'impossible', but I chose to disregard that 'impossibility' and hang on to the belief that with God, all things are possible. I firmly believe that what needs to change in order to release our potential is our thinking. When your chances of prevailing are against the odds, don't quit, but press on and choose to believe that it is impossible for the odds to stop you.

Don't ever let criticism and harsh words get you down. When you start to believe what others say about you, then you are in serious trouble. I get called all sorts of names. One that I have mentioned in this book is 'steroid monkey'. Much as I loathe being accused of taking steroids, I have to live with this. I have a choice: I can choose either to let it affect me or to move beyond it. I choose to move beyond and not let it affect me. In life you have to choose between being a 'thermometer' and a 'thermostat' kind of person.

The mercury in a thermometer works by changing according to the temperature of its surroundings. A thermostat, on the other hand, is set at a specific temperature and brings its surrounding environment to that temperature.

Do you understand my point? Don't be a 'thermometer' person, fluctuating according to the surroundings and easily influenced by the environment. Rather choose to be a 'thermostat' person, constant and true and unyielding when exposed to pressures from the environment. I admit that in my early days I used to be a 'thermometer' person, but now I like to believe that I am a 'thermostat' person. There is Proverb I really like that says,

As a man thinks in his heart, so is he![40]

What this tells me is that if you think, 'It can't be done,' or 'I can't do it,' then the chances are you will achieve precisely nothing. On the other hand, if you can conceive your goal in your mind and promote it with a positive attitude, then you are giving yourself every chance of achieving it. Within you are seeds of great potential – seeds that, I hope, have sprung to life as you have read this book. The main thing I want you to remember is that the quality of your life is determined by the quality of your choices. As successful businesswoman Jean Nidetch said,

It's choice – not chance – that determines your destiny.

By making wise choices you can unlock the potential within you. You probably won't achieve your dreams overnight; it will take time and discipline. My dad always said that if you want to change, then you have to start to do things differently. You cannot expect different results if you keep doing the same things. Change sometimes doesn't happen overnight, but you have to start to want to change. It all begins with the first step. The great basketball player Michael Jordan always approached everything one step at a time in his quest to achieve his goals. He advises:

Take those small steps ... All those steps are like pieces of a puzzle. They all come together to form a picture ... Step by step, I can't see any other way of accomplishing anything.

Looking to the future may fill some people with a lot of uncertainty, but while we may not know what the future holds, we can take comfort in Him who holds the future, God Almighty. Having a close relationship with Jesus Christ makes me understand that, like Corrie ten Boom, I must 'never be afraid to trust an unknown future to a known God'!

I know that my rugby career will eventually come to an end, as do most things in life. Don't get me wrong, my rugby is important to me, but if I had to lose it, it wouldn't mean my life going down the drain. I almost lost it twice, with my broken arm and blood clots, but God gave me another chance.

So what does the future hold for Pierre Spies after rugby? I would like to think that I would go into our 'family business' and fulfil the calling that came to my missionary grandfather, which I believe now rests upon my life. When my grandfather had completed his commerce studies in the 1940s at the University of Potchefstroom, he was challenged by God with this question:

Whom shall I send?

After rugby I may just take up that call and say, 'Me, Lord, send me!' Whatever it is, I know for sure that my life doesn't belong to me, but to God. He is the reason I live and have breath, so I want to do everything to live a life that is pleasing to Him. My dad's message of hope always rings loudly:

THE BEST IS YET TO COME, ALWAYS!

FINAL WORD
BY DEIRDRE SPIES –
MY MUM

I do not see myself as knowing all the answers. Neither am I an expert on how to raise godly children. Whatever I know I am thankful to God for, through His Word.

As Pierre was growing up, there were a few times when his life was in danger. When I was five months pregnant with him, I could have lost him, as his life was threatened by a growth that was growing much faster than he was in my womb. The doctor told us that a miscarriage was inevitable, as it was impossible to operate. My father-in-law, Pastor Spies, prayed for our unborn baby and asked God to spare his life for His glory. When I went back to the doctors, miraculously there was no sign of the growth. We knew it was from the hand of God, and so did the doctor!

On another occasion Pierre got lost on the farm – only 18 months old, not able to talk or answer when he was called. He took to the fields, as he was intrigued with the cattle. All the neighbouring farmers and workers looked for him, and we found him after some time – it seemed like hours – in the middle of a herd of cattle, only a few metres away from the big champion Brahman bull!

The third time he was only two years old. We were visiting family and he was swimming with his cousins. His father and the rest of the family were sitting close to the pool, keeping an eye on the children. All of a sudden they realised that Pierre was missing, and then they saw him on the floor of the pool. Pierre's dad jumped over the fence. (He was Africa record holder in the 110-metre hurdles.) Fortunately my uncle, who is a doctor, was also there and could administer CPR so that once again God miraculously saved Pierre's life.

It is said that 'when the father dies, the son becomes a man'. That is exactly what happened when Pierre's dad passed away in 2000. From that moment, Pierre took over his dad's role and all the responsibility that went with being 'the man in the house'. Just as his dad used to send us SMSs and flowers, Pierre would do the same. Despite being only 19 years old, he focused from that moment on filling his dad's shoes.

It would seem that his dad prepared him for this role from a young age. His passing away so soon was probably part of a bigger plan. Before Pierre's dad died, he wrote me a letter saying that the Lord had spoken to him and said he would be taken 'home' soon. In a way he may have had a premonition that his time on earth would be short, and that is why he prepared Pierre and motivated and encouraged him to succeed him.

My late husband, Pierre Snr, planted so many good seeds in the people around him, and in hindsight they could not grow unless he passed on. I have met so many people who have testified to the great influence for good he had on their lives. His brothers were like small plants in the shadow of a big tree, and when he was taken away, they were allowed to grow. It's the same with Pierre, because his career took off soon after his dad passed away. I believe his job of preparing Pierre to take over had been accomplished. There is a verse that says,

> Unless a grain of wheat falls into the ground and dies, it remains alone; but if it dies, it produces much grain.[41]

Pierre's dad had an amazing anointing and gifting on his life, and I believe that this has rubbed off onto Pierre. Even though Pierre's dad and I divorced, I always maintained that he was the man I wanted to grow old with and believed that we would get back together one day. My upbringing taught me to walk in truth and be truthful in all aspects of life. It's easier to live with the truth and the consequences of that than to live with a lie. I despise anything to do with pretence, and that is why I raised my kids to stay true to themselves:

Don't lie to yourself, and be the best you can be!

It is important for me that 'what you see is what you get'. I firmly believe that 'I cannot give you the measles if I have got the mumps'. People can only get what you have got, and this is what I instilled in Pierre. He needs to be an example in all aspects of his life, and not just talk it but live it. There are times in life when your faith is tested, and my advice is: keep on keeping on, even when dark times come; remember, it is only for a season. Pierre mentioned the tough financial times we went through. At that time I used to remind the kids that we had to believe and trust in God that this would all pass. I used to share this saying of Gregory Peck's with them:

Tough times don't last, tough people do, remember?

I also taught the kids to never see themselves as 'victims', but instead to take responsibility for their own lives. We have a tendency to blame others for what happens in our lives. The sooner we come to the realisation that we and no one else are accountable for our lives, the sooner we will start to move ahead. If you really want to achieve something, then you will not allow excuses to stand in your way. Your environment and your peers are not an excuse for making wrong choices.

As a mother I am really proud of Pierre and all that God has allowed him to achieve thus far. He is an example to his sisters and me, and his faith in God has also strengthened us in our lives. He was really concerned for Johanni and never gave up on her. He kept praying for her and inviting her to church. When she saw the positive changes in his life, she also recommitted her life to God. She wanted what he had, because she saw the favour of God on his life.

Although our family went through a very difficult time with the divorce, we always had a close bond. God can take our mess and turn it into a message! What we may think of as a setback is really a set-up for a greater comeback.

I tried to teach my children the importance of communication, and to be considerate to each other.

- Always live in truth.
- Be led by integrity and uprightness – even if it's all you have.
- Keep on keeping on, even when nobody is there to applaud you.
- In every situation, no matter how daunting or how difficult, remember: this too shall pass.
- Forget the past and move forward. We only have today. Make the best of what you have.
- Take responsibility for your circumstances. Always do your best.
- Trust in God. God is in control.

When Pierre suffered the misfortune of blood clots in his lungs, we witnessed first-hand the peace of God in his life. You can imagine the pain I felt as a mother when my son, who I knew had worked so hard to get to the World Cup in 2007, had to face all of this. As a mum, my heart went out to him. Pierre, despite the turmoil and uncertainty that he faced, was rooted in his faith. At a time when he confronted so much disappointment, he was a witness and comfort to us, just in the way he carried himself through this tough time. He would come home and lock his door, and then we would hear him worshipping and singing praises to God and praying.

His circumstances didn't change him or, more importantly, who God was in his life. It's easy to praise God when things are going well, but Pierre showed us what it meant to 'bring a sacrifice of praise' and how to live our lives in glory to God. He didn't allow himself to be angry with God. He was calm and at peace, because he had chosen not to allow this illness to overcome him, but instead to overcome it. He would tell us that God was in control, calm us down, and share this verse to encourage us:

We are more than overcomers through Christ who strengthens us.

As his mum it gives me great pleasure to have written this 'final word' for my son, Pierre Spies. He was a child given to me by God to raise up in

His ways. I knew that he would not belong to me, but to God and the greater calling he has over his life. Pierre's life is destined for bigger things, and I know that the best is yet to come. My prayer for Pierre and all my children is that God will bless them with spiritual wisdom to make wise decisions and that they may fulfil their God-given destiny. God is faithful, and when we come to Him and ask His forgiveness to redeem us from all our mistakes, He sees our hearts and knows our motives. As you have read this book, maybe certain parts of it have touched you. Maybe you are in need of hope or are going through a tough time and need comfort and peace. May I suggest that you get hold of a Bible and begin to read the words and teachings of Jesus Christ, who is the solid rock that my son, Pierre, bases his life on. I can assure you there is great encouragement, comfort and peace to be found within its pages.

Only one life, 'twill soon be past, only what's done for Christ will last.

God bless,

Deirdre Spies

APPENDIX

Overview of Pierre Spies's achievements

2002	Craven Week – lock	
2003	Craven Week No. 8 – captain, Affies 1st team captain	
2004	SA U/19 – wing Suffered serious arm injury in quarter-final against France; out injured for rest of year	
2005	Youngest player to play Super 12, with debut at 19 SA Students team Tuks University Carlton League Blue Bulls U/21 top try scorer – 9 tries in 6 games	
2006	Blue Bulls Super 14 SA U/21 Springbok debut – Australia v South Africa in Brisbane Man of the match – NZ v South Africa in Rustenburg	SA most promising player of the year SA Currie Cup player of the year nominee SA player of the year nominee International new player of the year nominee
2007	Team member Bulls Super 14 winners Springbok man of the match – SA v England in Pretoria Selected for Springbok World Cup team – withdrew for medical reasons	
2008	Returned from illness Bulls Super 14 squad Springbok squad	
2009	Bulls Super 14 winners Springboks – winners of series against British and Irish Lions Bulls Currie Cup winners Super 14 player of the year nominee	
2010	Bulls Super 14 winners	Springbok squad

A NOTE FROM THE WRITER
BY MYAN SUBRAYAN

Given the almost impossible circumstances, completing this book was in itself an accomplishment. These pages tell a story of immense inspiration and motivation about a truly blessed individual, Pierre Spies. Our connection and coming together to make this book possible can only be described as a miracle – from the time I read about his victory over blood clots in 2009 to our first meeting in Auckland in April 2010, and then to January 2011, when we finally started work on the manuscript. I firmly believe this was possible only through divine assistance, plain and simple. Pierre's tremendous commitment to seeing this project completed also needs mentioning, as well as the support I received from his immediate family in putting this book together. My heartfelt thanks to the Spies family for sharing what they have to make this book even more special to all who read it.

I am truly humbled and privileged to have been given the opportunity to play a part in putting this together. The process of working on the manuscript with Pierre was certainly uplifting and encouraging for me, and I know that the reader will be similarly blessed. *Pierre Spies: More than Rugby* – is a source of tremendous hope and encouragement, which I believe will inspire all who read it. It is a reminder to us to always make lemonade when the world throws us lemons – never to get bitter, but to get better by choosing to never give up!

To God be the glory!

Born in Durban, South Africa, **Myan Subrayan** *emigrated to New Zealand in 2000, where he resides in Auckland with his wife, Jolene, and four daughters.* He is the co-author of former All Black Inga Tuigamala's recent autobiography, Inga: My Story, *and has authored his own books,* From the Pit to the Palace, You Can *and* Half Black to All Black. *Myan Subrayan is a life coach, corporate trainer, pastor and motivational speaker who also helps others pen their stories. He is passionate about helping people live to their maximum potential.*

For more info visit www.hope2overcome.org and www.myansubrayan.com

ENDNOTES

Key to Bible translations used
ESV   English Standard Version
KJV   King James Version
NASB   New American Standard Bible
NIV   New International Version
NKJV   New King James Version
NLT   New Living Translation

1. 1 Thessalonians 3:12 (Adapted from NLT)

2. Proverbs 3:1-10 (NLT)

3. NKJV

4. Matthew Knight (2009) *Between the Lines: The Spirit of South African Rugby*. Johannesburg: Penguin (p 31).

5. Matthew Knight (2009) *Between the Lines: The Spirit of South African Rugby*. Johannesburg: Penguin (pp ix, x).

6. On holding the wall: you literally stand with your arms on the wall as if you are pushing it. Like pushing a broken-down car! So the matrics would shout at us for not pushing hard enough, which was hard as there was not alot of space, so we had to find space, next to another new Grade 8 student that you didn't even know as yet! That's the first part of the initiation. I remember a guy walking past telling me how small my calves were and truthfully he wasn't far from wrong. But race horses dont have calves, do they?

7. This is a book that I strongly encourage you to read. It is based on this verse:

    And Jabez called on the God of Israel saying, 'Oh, that You would bless me indeed, and enlarge my territory, that Your hand would be with me, and that You would keep me from evil, that I may not cause pain.' So God granted him what he requested. (I Chronicles 4:10 NKJV)

8. Isaiah 55:10–11 (NKJV)

9. Jim Rohn

10. Henry Ford

11. John 10:10

12. Deuteronomy 30:19 (NIV)

13. 'For I hate divorce!' says the LORD, the God of Israel. 'To divorce your wife is to overwhelm her with cruelty,' says the LORD of Heaven's Armies. 'So guard your heart; do not be unfaithful to your wife.' (Malachi 2:16, NLT)

14. Dr David Popenoe, author of *Life Without Father: Compelling New Evidence that Fatherhood and Marriage are Indispensable to the Good of Children and Society.* New York: Free Press

15. Psalm 139: 13–16 (NLT)

16. Ecclesiastes 9:11 (NIV)

17. Kamp Staaldraad ('Camp Barbed Wire' in English) was a military-style boot camp organised as a 'team-building' exercise for the Springboks during their preparation for the 2003 Rugby World Cup. It was very controversial because some of the training, according to press leaks, required the players to be naked.

18. John 13:7 (NIV)

19. 1 Corinthians 15:33 (NIV)

20. Va'aiga Tuigamala with Myan Subrayan (2009) *Inga: My Story.* Auckland: Penguin (p 197)

21. Malachi 4:6 (NKJV)

22. NASB

23. Proverbs 16:7 (ESV)

24. Proverbs 3:11–12 (NKJV)

25. Hebrews 12:7–11 (NLT)

26. Jeremiah 29:11 (NIV)

27. Romans 8:28 (KJV)

28. Job 1:21–22 (NKJV)

29. Job 2:9–10 (NKJV)

30. G K Chesterton

31. Hebrews 13:5 (NKJV)

32. Job 13:15 (NKJV

33. Job 42:10 (NKJV)

34. Job 42:5 (NKJV)

35. Jeremiah 29:11 (ESV)

36. John Maxwell

37. Genesis 2:24 (NKJV)

38. These statistics are provided by Focus on the Family South Africa and come from an article published in 2008 entitled 'Marriage' by Focus on the Family Issue Analysts.

39. Benjamin Scafidi, *The Taxpayer Costs of Divorce and Unwed Childbearing*, http://www.americanvalues.org/pdfs/COFF.pdf

40. Proverbs 23:7 (Adapted from NKJV)

41. John 12:24 (NKJV)